TOLERANCE AND THE ETHICAL LIFE

Continuum Studies in Philosophy:
Series Editor: James Fieser, University of Tennessee at Martin

TOLERANCE AND THE ETHICAL LIFE

ANDREW FIALA

continuum
LONDON • NEW YORK

Continuum
The Tower Building, 11 York Road, London SE1 7NX
15 East 26th Street, New York, NY 10010

British Library Cataloguing-in-Publication Data
A catalogue record for this book is available from the British Library.

ISBN: HB: 0–8264–7844–1

Library of Congress Cataloging-in-Publication Data
A catalog record for this book is available from the Library of Congress.

Typeset by Aarontype Limited, Easton, Bristol
Printed and bound in Great Britain by Antony Rowe Ltd, Chippenham, Wilts

CONTENTS

ACKNOWLEDGEMENTS

Several of the chapters in the present volume were previously published as journal articles. A version of Chapter 3 originally appeared as 'Toleration and the limits of the moral imagination' in *Philosophy in the Contemporary World*, 10:2 (Fall–Winter 2003), 33–40; it is reprinted here with permission. A version of Chapter 4 originally appeared as 'Stoic tolerance' in *Res Publica*, 9:2 (2003), 149–68; it is reprinted here with permission. A version of Chapter 6 originally appeared as 'Existential and repressive toleration' in *Studies in Practical Philosophy*, 6:2 (Fall 2004); it is reprinted here with permission. A version of Chapter 8 originally appeared as 'Pragmatism and liberalism' in *Journal of Speculative Philosophy*, 16:2 (2002), 103–16; it is reprinted here with permission. Some of the ideas presented here also appear in my article on 'Toleration' in the *Internet Encyclopedia of Philosophy*.

I would especially like to acknowledge the support and criticism of Trudy Conway, Joe Frank Jones III, Derek Jeffreys, John Lachs, Rob Metcalf and Hye-Kyung Kim.

1
Philosophy and the Virtue of Tolerance

Toleration, as a political principle, has enjoyed enormous success in the modern West. But tolerance, as a virtue of the ethical life for individuals, is an ancient idea. Modern Western societies have institutionalized the ideas that state power should be limited, that dissent should be protected and that conformity is not necessary for social stability. But the idea that we should allow others the freedom to discover the truth for themselves has been with us since Socrates. The Socratic model of ethical life assumes that knowledge produces virtue and that genuine knowledge cannot be produced by coercion. This model of the ethical life links philosophical practice with the pursuit of virtue together with others in a tolerant community of dialogue. This model provides the historical inspiration for the contemporary ideal of political toleration.

Intolerance is a form of hubris that condemns and destroys what is not understood. Instead of inspiring questions, the intolerant aim to stifle debate; instead of provoking wonder, they mask uncertainty with fanaticism. Tolerance results from a modest, self-critical understanding of human limitations. Tolerant thinkers are not afraid to admit their ignorance or uncertainty. Tolerance is thus grounded in wonder and self-restraint. Tolerance requires us to aim beyond our particular loyalties towards a higher critical view from which we might see the loyalties of others as worthy of respect. Philosophical education is the ladder that leads us to this tolerant vantage point.

Tolerance is a virtue that is closely allied with other virtues such as modesty, generosity and hospitality.[1] Tolerance, as a virtue, is thus not a form of passive indifference. Rather, it is a positive value linked to other values that allow for human flourishing. The vision of the tolerant ethical life emphasizes the value of the pursuit of wisdom within communities of difference. The tolerant community is one in which participants recognize the limits of knowledge and share a commitment to engage together in the process of questioning, while allowing one another to disagree. This recognition of difference within the community shows us why tolerance is a difficult virtue. The easy traditional response to the fact of diversity is to destroy it, thus ensuring conformity through the use of violence. The more difficult, tolerant approach works through diversity by using dialogue to uncover values that are shared despite difference. Tolerance is, then, a virtue of what we might call tragic communities. These are communities of those who do not have everything in common. All communities involve conflict: even our most intimate and loving relations with others involve moments of disagreement. Unless we are willing to use violence to resolve conflict, tolerance will be required. But tolerance involves a sacrifice. Individuals cannot share a life in common without giving up something of value. And tolerance requires us to sacrifice the comfortable sense of self-certainty that is found in closed communities.

Tolerant communities are fragile and precarious: they are always at risk from the dogmatic and fanatical forces of intolerance. The example of Socrates shows us the dangers that are encountered whenever the tolerant voice of philosophy is confronted by the dogmatic voices of political and/or religious self-assurance. The voice of philosophy should be tolerant and cautious, guided by questions and restrained by modesty. But the voice of politics (and sometimes religion) is often arrogant and reckless, grounded in authority and inflamed by fanaticism. The opposition between modesty and tolerance, on the one hand, and arrogance and intolerance, on the other, is not only a difference in tone and style but also involves a different mode of self-understanding. Ultimately it is an opposition between different conceptions of the relation between power, truth and freedom. The dogmatic and intolerant want power and are not afraid to utilize violence to achieve the end of establishing certainty beyond doubt. The modest and tolerant want truth and genuine consensus. They are wary of the violence of pride and they are reluctant to utilize methods that violate the freedom of others. This puts the tolerant at an immediate disadvantage in struggles against fanaticism and intolerance. The tolerant philosopher approaches the proud dogmatist and arrogant fanatic with questions and doubts. But the intolerant often reply with threats, weapons, prisons and worse.

It might seem that, in the West at least, the spirit of tolerance is prevailing. But such historical pronouncements are fraught with uncertainty. Tolerance faces external threats in the guise of terrorists and other intolerant fanatics. But tolerance also faces internal threats. On the one hand, some have argued that intolerance is inscribed in the heart of Western thinking.[2] On the other hand, the tolerant occasionally misunderstand tolerance, thus leaving them unable to defend it. This book will argue against both of these internal threats. I will show that the Western tradition has a deep core commitment to tolerance. And I will provide reasons why tolerance is good. The problem of the external threat to toleration indicates the limits of philosophy: philosophy does not provide the material weapons needed to battle against intolerance, fanaticism and dogmatism. This leaves philosophy in a precarious position, as I will show by examining, in this chapter, what we can learn from the case of Socrates.

Tolerance and open-minded philosophical inquiry are fragile products of the human spirit, whose delicate flower only blossoms in the right circumstances. Just as the human spirit contains the capacity to love wisdom and pursue open inquiry, it also contains the rival tendency towards a form of self-satisfaction that closes minds and spawns intolerance. The best way to fend off this intolerant tendency is to describe the beauty of the philosophical life and to show the strength that flows from the virtue of tolerance.

The Socratic model

Socrates is the tragic hero of the philosophical life and his model is central to what I will discuss in the following chapters.[3] Socrates' philosophical practice was seen as an affront to established power. His commitment to the goods of philosophy ultimately cost him his life. The potential for tragedy remains wherever the fragile spirit of inquiry is confronted by those who want unanimity and who are not afraid to use force to establish it. But the example of Socrates continues to inspire us to cultivate tolerance and to create philosophical communities, even in the face of intolerance. Socratic inquiry is interested in a genuine foundation for belief and for community. For Socrates, and for all subsequent philosophers worthy of the name, wisdom is not established by coercive force; rather, it is developed through tolerant dialogue. But the tolerant love of wisdom is always at risk from those who are willing to use violence to enforce conformity.

The basic assumption of the history that I tell in this book is that tolerance is a requirement for finite mortal human beings who are engaged in the quest to discover truth and who enjoy the process of creating a community of inquiry out of the diversity of human life. I associate this view with what I call philosophy. Philosophy is an art of wondering that includes wondering about philosophy itself. In other words, philosophy is a discipline that calls itself into question. This idea derives from the Socratic idea that 'the unexamined life is not worth living'. If we take this claim seriously, then we must admit that even it can be questioned. This is not to say that the claim is unjustified. Indeed, it is hard to imagine a claim that is better justified. Rather, the point is that even this Socratic first principle is subject to constant critical self-evaluation. This modest, self-critical stance is closely related to the spirit of tolerance. Tolerance develops from the conviction that all convictions can be questioned – even this one. The tolerant are open to an educational process that asks them to wonder whether their convictions are in fact justified. One of the difficulties of tolerance, as we shall see, is to prevent this spirit of wonder from becoming a pernicious form of scepticism.

Tolerance is related to the virtue that the Greeks called *sophrosyne*. This can be translated as 'moderation' or 'temperance'. Socrates discusses this in the *Charmides*, where one of the definitions he considers is 'doing your own business'.[4] As the dialogue proceeds we discover that in order to mind your own business you need to know what your own business is. The *Charmides* thus shows us the importance of the quest for self-knowledge as well as providing us with an example of how this quest and indeed the virtue of sophrosyne operate. The dialogue ends with an indication of the spirit of tolerance. Socrates tells Charmides that he must begin again to examine himself to discover whether he is in fact temperate because temperance and self-examination go hand in hand. But Charmides admits that he does not know what temperance is and mockingly threatens Socrates with violence: the violent demand to teach him further. The difficulty presented here is twofold. On the one hand, moderation requires immoderate devotion to philosophy. On the other, although moderation requires self-knowledge, self-knowledge only develops through moderation. Thus we need to constantly question ourselves and one another to ensure that we are actually temperate for the right reasons. And we cannot be moderate about our devotion to moderation. The same sorts of problems apply with regard to tolerance. We cannot be tolerant towards intolerance; and we must continually examine tolerance in a spirit of tolerance in order to know if tolerance is actually good.

In the *Charmides*, Socrates expresses his dream of a perfect state in which everyone would be perfectly temperate – a dream expanded in the *Republic*. In this utopia, each would know his place and do his own business; and no one would 'pretend to know matters of which he is ignorant'.[5] This can be linked to tolerance if we realize that we should refrain from meddling with the business of others, about which we are ignorant. The problem is that, despite pretensions to knowledge, we are all ignorant. Socrates thus leaves us with a negative account: don't meddle with what you don't understand. Although the spirit of tolerance is stated negatively here, tolerance can be linked to positive engagement with others in dialogical inquiry into the very question of whether and why tolerance is good. The truly tolerant utopia is the philosophical community.

It should be noted that Socrates finds it difficult to give positive arguments for his ethical ideal. As Nehamas concludes: 'Socrates' invitation to his interlocutors is protreptic and non-dogmatic. His attitude is moderate: he wants people to follow his new way of life but has no arguments to convince them they must do so.'[6] One of the difficulties of tolerance is that the spirit of tolerance seems to leave us without the capacity to make positive arguments against the intolerant in favour of tolerance. One solution is to model an ethical life committed to tolerance, rather than argue for it. Indeed Socrates can be looked to as such a model. But, it seems to me, such models do contain implicit arguments, even though they can mix ethical, religious and aesthetic elements. One of my goals in subsequent chapters is to make the implicit argument for tolerance more explicit.

The model of Socrates' tolerant life reaches its climax in the speech in the *Apology* in which he defends himself before the Athenian assembly. Socrates' trial occurred in the context of disillusionment, doubt and self-recrimination within Athens after Athens had lost the Peloponnesian war. Indeed, Greek society at this time was characterized by cultural turmoil and religious pluralism.[7] Criticism of the Socratic method was a natural focal point for those who were dissatisfied with the confusion of this era. Social conservatives did not want to tolerate alternative beliefs. And they prosecuted Socrates in an attempt to preserve the purity and integrity of traditional society.

Unlike these intolerant conservatives, Socrates confronted everyone – both those with alternative beliefs and those with traditional beliefs – in a tolerant manner, engaging them in dialogue in the hope of discovering some truth to which both he and his interlocutors could agree. He even does this in the heart of his defence speech as he interrogates Meletus, one of his accusers. In general, when agreement is not forthcoming, Socrates allows his opponents to go their own way. He does not resort to violence or employ other tactics such as shamefully pleading for his life. For Socrates, the goal is not merely to win the argument but to understand himself and his interlocutors. Unlike his political opponents, Socrates is not willing to condemn the activities of another without first seeking to understand them. When it turns out that the ideas or activities of another are inconsistent or not understandable, Socrates does not resort to violence or active intervention. Rather, he utilizes dialectic as his instrument of criticism.

The difficulty exposed here is that the spirit of tolerance leaves Socrates vulnerable to intolerant political power. It makes sense to say that Socrates *tolerates* the verdict of the Athenians, as well as the sentence imposed upon him. This is explained, in part, in the *Crito*, where Socrates tells us that 'the really important thing is not to live, but to live well.'[8] This leads to the implication that we should tolerate threats to our lives out of concern for higher goods. Ultimately Socrates argues that the higher good requires him to tolerate the decision of the city. At one point in the *Crito*, the Laws of the city appear to Socrates in a vision and claim that they are one of the most venerable entities known to man. And they conclude, 'If you cannot persuade your country, you must do whatever it orders and patiently submit (*hêsuchian agonta*) to any punishment it imposes.'[9] The idea of gently or quietly undergoing is quite close to the idea of toleration. The choice presented here is thus either to tolerate or to persuade. Thus the Laws rule out the legitimacy of other options such as escape or even more extreme options that would employ violence. It should be clear that these two options – persuade or tolerate – work together in the spirit of philosophy: philosophers tolerate others and seek to persuade them; but they do not use other means to effect change. In the political context, we thus see the fragility and limit of tolerance. Socrates tolerates the verdict because he has not been able to persuade the city otherwise and is not willing to employ other means to affect the outcome.

Socratic tolerance may appear to be politically naïve. At least, it is obvious that tolerance of this sort is best suited for private encounters between individuals. We see Socrates enact tolerance, for example, in his private conversation with Euthyphro. The dialogue with Euthyphro concludes with Socrates asking Euthyphro, who is befuddled by his own circular reasoning, to begin again with another attempt to define piety. Euthyphro, however, breaks the dialogue off and claims that he is in a hurry to go somewhere. Socrates tolerantly allows him to leave. This motif of breaking off the dialogue occurs in many places in the Socratic dialogues: the most famous example is probably Socrates' confrontation with Thrasymachus in the *Republic*. This usually indicates that the interlocutor has reached the limit of his toleration for Socrates' inquiry. In a sense, the interlocutor who leaves the dialogical space has indicated that he may resort to the sorts of material weapons that have no place in the dialogue. It is interesting that Socrates, however, tolerantly allows his opponents to break off. He does not force them to change their minds or chase them down and badger them into submission. He does not pursue them further and does not force them to go deeper or farther than they are willing to go. It makes sense to say, then, that Socrates tolerates Euthyphro's disregard for the customs of filial piety, for Socrates does nothing further to prevent Euthyphro from going forward with his case. And yet the hope is that Socrates has planted the seed of doubt that leads to the process of self-knowledge.

This hope is fragile and perhaps unfounded. Socrates' tolerance is thus always risky: in permitting his opponents to leave the philosophical community, he risks having them destroy that community from the outside. One imagines with horror a scene in which a disgruntled interlocutor returns with a real weapon and expresses his intolerance with the force of arms. The *Apology* shows us how political reality eventually invades and destroys the philosophical space in a very real way: the vote of the Athenian assembly asserts the violent means available to the political community. The *Symposium* offers another example, in which Alcibiades bursts into the room in a drunken frenzy. But Alcibiades is a lover of Socrates, who, despite his consternation with Socrates, recognizes the rules that govern the dialogical space: he can mock Socrates with words but he cannot resort to physical coercion.

Unfortunately violent intolerance is easy enough to imagine in a world in which fanatics are willing to kill in the name of their ideas. Genuine philosophical communities are thus more difficult to imagine. This is why we need to read the Platonic dialogues: they inspire us with models of tolerant dialogue. When the dialogue is genuine, we see the formation of a community of inquiry. In the *Lysis*, for example, Socrates and his companions engage in a dialogue about friendship that provides an example of what friendship truly is. The dialogue concludes with Socratic ignorance as Socrates says to Lysis and Menexenus that although they are friends, they do not know what friendship is. However, friendship is exactly what we witness in the dialogue: a genuine concern with one another as they struggle together to understand friendship. And this friendship is tolerant yet critical: the interlocutors are responsive and responsible as they work together to push back the bounds of their own ignorance. This dialogue is an inspiring example of a philosophical community of inquiry. It is wonderful indeed to share a rare and blessed occasion of communing with friends or lovers wondering together about the very fact that they are friends.

And yet, as we see in the *Lysis*, such philosophical communities are tragic. They exist for a moment and often reach no concrete conclusion. And they are always threatened with dissolution from without. In the *Lysis*, the dialogical community is destroyed by the attendants of Lysis and Menexenus, who as Socrates says, 'came down upon us like beings from another world'.[10] At a certain point, the 'real' world – the 'other' world outside the dialogical space – intrudes and the dialogue must come to an end. Nonetheless, the activity of philosophizing, if only for a few moments, can inspire us to continue to develop such fragile and fleeting communities. What is important about such moments is the process of philosophizing itself – not the answers developed. This process helps to develop and strengthen those philosophical virtues such as tolerance that, when the dialogue is over, we can bring with us to the rest of our lives. Thus, despite the instability of philosophical communities, the spirit of the philosophical community can be used as the model for our more concrete communities in the 'real' world.

Unfortunately, such philosophical communities and the practice of tolerant questioning upon which they are founded run counter to the interests of traditional political and religious authorities. The *Apology* makes explicit the tension between Socratic inquiry and traditional values, the tension between tolerant criticism and intolerant self-assurance. In a culture that is in turmoil, Socratic communities seem to promise only more uncertainty and even disillusionment, all in the name of enlightenment and virtue. The Athenian polis was not, however, willing to tolerate this. The intolerant solution of the majority of the Athenian assembly was to stifle questioning, diversity and doubt by silencing the voice of philosophy. During political crises, diversity and doubt can look like enemies of the people. The best way to congeal the spirit of the community at such times is to set up dissenters as examples to the masses of what happens to those who are not compliant.

Socrates was not unaware of the problem of politics. When Socrates commits himself to the philosophical life by saying that the 'unexamined life is not worth living', he admits that he will not be able to persuade some members of his audience about this point.[11] This is true, in part, because Socrates refuses to use the rhetorical ploys of his accusers. But Socrates also seems to realize that acceptance of the philosophical life is a choice involving all our human interests: aesthetic, ethical, religious and philosophical. He thus ends his apologia with a description of the way of life of philosophy as carried over into the afterlife. For Socrates, the philosopher will be rewarded in death with the opportunity to engage in dialogue in the world of the dead. But this idea of continuing to do philosophy will obviously not appeal to those who find no joy in philosophy. Thus the argument for philosophy will only appeal to those who are inspired by the idea of spending eternity puzzling tolerantly over truth. Such a description of the 'reward' of doing philosophy will not appeal to those who want final answers and who envision the afterlife as leading to the end of philosophizing in the final beatific vision of truth.

The choice of such a philosophical life is not an easy one to make. And it is not obvious that this life is a good one. We should not forget the allure of the idea that final answers can be obtained and that differences can be overcome. Human beings are torn between two rival forces: one seeking unity, security and an end to doubt; and another seeking risk, freedom and new ideas. Our ambivalence occasionally leads to the triumph of intolerance as we succumb to our desire for security. However, those of us inspired by the tolerant spirit of philosophical questioning are not willing to stifle our doubts and repress our questions. We are not willing to conform without critically engaging the ideals to which we are supposed to conform. We are not willing to sacrifice the pursuit of truth for the stability of truth obtained. And we tolerate others because we enjoy the challenge of confronting diversity in pursuit of community. But we must acknowledge that the Socratic way of life reaches its limit when it confronts intolerant political power.

Philosophy and scepticism

One of the problems of philosophy is that it is an art, which must, like other arts, be transmitted and taught in the context of a community of practitioners. By art, here, I mean something like what MacIntyre has described as a 'practice': a set of social activities that define virtues or standards of excellence.[12] The virtue of tolerance is thus defined within the communal practice that is philosophy. Most philosophers think that the virtues of the philosophical life are virtues of human beings as such and not merely virtues of philosophers. But as philosophers since Socrates have known, the philosophical virtues are not widely accepted. Enlightenment thinkers held out the hope that such virtues – including tolerance – could become widely disseminated. But this is, as yet, a dream. Moreover, as MacIntyre has shown, the dream of enlightenment is tragic insofar as the values of enlightenment inevitably clash with more traditional values.

It is important to remember that this is a genuinely tragic conflict. Real goods are provided by intolerant closed communities. There is real comfort to be found in dogmatic certainty. And fanaticism continues to have a psychological appeal. So when we argue in favour of tolerance, we must recognize that we are asking our opponents to sacrifice real goods. The philosopher's task is to remain committed, as Socrates did, to the virtues of the philosophical life when confronting the wide world of dogmatism and fanaticism. But we may learn to be more modest – and indeed more tolerant – when we recognize the sorts of good that are sacrificed in the name of tolerance. We may hope that philosophical virtues such as tolerance will spread. But this hope must not make us naïve about the depth of the conflict between tolerance and its other. Indeed, to ignore the depth of this conflict may in fact be to suffer from a form of hubris that is itself fanatical.

We learn the discipline of philosophy in community with others in the same way that we learn other arts or practices. We develop the philosophical virtues when they spread to us from the model provided by more experienced practitioners. The difficulty is, however, one of conversion: to convince a non-philosophical audience that philosophical virtues are good; to inspire tolerance in the intolerant. The norm of critical self-consciousness leads the philosopher to be tolerant towards his audience. But this form of philosophical tolerance often does not succeed in persuading an audience that is accustomed to listening only to the persuasive techniques of the fanatical and dogmatic. Thus tolerance is always at risk in its confrontation with its other.

This problem is exacerbated by a tendency to equate tolerance with relativism and to link philosophy with scepticism. The problem of scepticism and its risks for living well has haunted philosophy since Socrates claimed that the only thing he knew was that he knew nothing. Socratic doubt is a methodological first principle that demands that we be critically self-conscious. This is a normative claim that defines good thinking: good thinking is critically self-conscious, even up to the point that good thinking is aware of the limits of its own norms. This is why tolerance can and should be linked to critical engagement with others and not to indifference, as I shall argue in Chapter 2.

A defining trait of philosophy is its self-consciousness of its own limits. This is the grounding commitment from which tolerance is developed. We learn to tolerate others when we understand the limits of the human capacity to understand self and others. This recognition of limits is key to the approaches to be described in what follows.

It is important to note that critical self-consciousness – consciousness of our own limits – does not undermine the norms of good thinking. Rather, awareness of limits is essential to good thinking. Critical self-consciousness recognizes that there are limits to knowledge. But recognition of these limits does not undermine knowledge. Indeed, these limits are constitutive of knowledge. Some postmodern critiques of the project of enlightenment set an impossibly high standard for knowledge (under the rubric of 'the God's-eye-view' or 'Truth with a capital T'). Then, with this straw man in place, such critics 'prove' that knowledge cannot exist. It is obviously true that fallible human beings cannot possess the God's-eye-view. But there are still many things that we can know with a large degree of certainty, short of 'Truth with a capital T'. No reasonable human being – most theists included – has ever claimed to possess this absolute vantage point. But this does not mean that these reasonable beings cannot make very plausible claims to knowledge.

One of these plausible claims is that tolerance is a virtue. Virtues are usually thought to fall as the mean or middle between two extremes or vices. One sort of vice opposed to tolerance is intolerance, dogmatism and fanaticism. At the other extreme, we find the vices of relativism and scepticism. The opposition of scepticism and relativism to tolerance may not be obvious at first because, in fact, tolerance is often mistaken for relativism or scepticism. But an adequate account of tolerance must struggle against both dogmatic fanaticism and sceptical relativism. The first task is perhaps easier because our post-enlightenment culture has tended to embrace an anti-dogmatic point of view. The struggle against intolerance and dogmatism continues to be important. However, it is much more difficult to distinguish tolerance from relativism because our culture often encourages relativism in the name of tolerance as a reaction against fanaticism.

Tolerance is found in the middle ground between dogmatism and relativism. This middle way is the heart of philosophy. Philosophy – as a method, as a practice, as a way of life – is dedicated to modest questioning, tolerant criticism and an end to both dogmatism and relativism. Philosophers seek the truth about the self and the world. This means that we must self-consciously recognize our limitations and our fragility. Philosophers realize that no human being has all the answers. We are not gods; we are mortal beings struggling for light in the midst of a world that is often dark and incomprehensible. Intolerant dogmatists refuse to recognize the shadows and doubts that haunt our lives and ironically keep themselves in the dark. Relativists deliberately dwell in the shadows and refuse to look beyond them to the light. But tolerant philosophers aim to see beyond the shadows to the light, while acknowledging lingering doubts about any final access to the truth. Recognizing our limitations, seeing the shadows that surround us, does not, however, mean we must retreat to absolute scepticism, relativism and nihilism. It is true after all that we are all limited mortal beings. This truth alone should be enough to get us started on the middle path that avoids both the closed door of dogmatism and the abyss of relativism.

This description of philosophy as a middle path is, of course, an ideal and an aspiration. It is based, in part, upon the model of Socrates, who is himself an ideal and aspiration – the product of Plato's literary imagination. But it is also based upon the concrete experience of the rightness of the middle path that can be found in any genuinely philosophical community. Whenever we discuss ideas non-dogmatically, with an eye open for truth, we are doing philosophy. Almost every human being has experienced the feeling of satisfaction, hope and spiritual energy that occurs when philosophical conversations erupt among friends whom we trust and who are themselves inspired by the philosophical task. A philosophical community of inquiry develops even when good friends disagree with one another, so long as we listen to one another tolerantly and critique one another in a spirit of truth-seeking. It is this basic experience of philosophical community, with its spiritually energy, that is the highest aspiration of philosophical practice.

We should recognize that such philosophical communities are fragile and tragic. These communities are essentially tragic. These are not communities of like-minded folk who share everything in common. Rather, such communities are based upon the fact of diversity. The joy of such a community is found in the activity of confronting others across difference. The dialogue that develops here does not reach easy conclusions. Indeed, in truly diverse communities, there may in fact be no conclusion to the dialogue. But this is the appeal of such a community to the philosopher. We want to be confronted with new and surprising ideas. But the founding virtues of the community create conditions that make it difficult to obtain the final communion of like-mindedness. And these communities are always at risk both from external forces of intolerance and from an internal inability to distinguish tolerance from relativism.

The philosophical community is an ideal that is haunted by the fact that none of us is perfectly moderate, wise or tolerant. Thus we are always susceptible to the vices that lurk on either side of the virtue of tolerance: our tendency to become dogmatic and our tendency to slip into relativism. An examination of models of tolerance can help to remind us of its value as we engage in the on-going process of self-examination in community with others. Plato tells us that philosophy is a discipline that can only be learned by apprenticeship: 'Acquaintance with it [the truth of philosophy] must come rather after a long period of attendance on instruction in the subject itself and of close companionship, when, suddenly, like a blaze kindled by a leaping spark, it is generated in the soul and at once becomes self-sustaining.'[13] Studies in the history of philosophy, such as the present one, can serve to generate such sparks by showing us the ways in which important philosophers thought. My intention, then, in describing the various ways in which the virtue of tolerance shows up in some often overlooked sources in the Western tradition is to remind us of the value of tolerance and its central place in the ethical life.

Notes

1. See Trudy Conway, 'Tolerance and Hospitality' in *Philosophy in the Contemporary World* (forthcoming).

2. John McCumber, 'Aristotle and the Metaphysics of Intolerance' in Mehdi Amin Razavi and David Ambuel (eds) *Philosophy, Religion, and the Question of Intolerance*, Albany, NY: State University of New York Press, 1997.

3. In what follows, when I speak of Socrates it will be the Socrates of the early dialogues that I have in mind – the tolerant philosopher of questions and aporias – and not the Platonic character who advocates the repressive regime of the philosopher–king. For a discussion of tolerance in connection with Socrates see Gerald M. Mara, 'Socrates and Liberal Toleration', *Political Theory*, 16:3 (August 1988), pp. 468–95.

4. Plato, *Charmides*, p. 161b. In the *Gorgias*, Socrates says that the philosopher 'who has applied himself to his own business and not played the busybody in his life' will be blessed in the afterlife (Plato, *Gorgias*, p. 526c). All quotes from Plato are from *The Collected Dialogues of Plato*, by Edith Hamilton and Huntington Cairns, Princeton, NJ: Princeton University Press, 1989. All subsequent references to the Platonic corpus refer to this collection.

5. Plato, *Charmides*, p. 173b.

6. Alexander Nehamas, *The Art of Living*, Berkeley, CA: University of California Press, 1998, p. 97.

7. See J.K. Davies, *Democracy and Classical Greece*, Stanford, CA: Stanford University Press, 1978, Chapter 9.

8. *Crito*, p. 48d.

9. *Crito*, p. 51b.

10. *Lysis*, p. 223 a.

11. Plato, *Apology*, p. 38a. I discuss the problem of politics for Socrates and Plato in Chapter 1 of *The Philosopher's Voice*, Albany, NY: State University of New York Press, 2002.

12. Alasdair MacIntyre, *After Virtue*, Notre Dame, IN: Notre Dame University Press, 1984.

13. Plato, *Letter: VII*, p. 341c.

2

Critical Moral Tolerance

Toleration requires a complex understanding of the self and its moral commitments. Our English word is derived from the Latin, *tolerantia*, which is associated with the general idea of enduring, suffering, bearing or putting up with.[1] Tolerance is generally used as a term to describe a virtue, characteristic or tendency to engage in acts of toleration. When we say, in our ordinary language, for example, that someone has a 'high tolerance for pain' we mean that he or she tends to be able to endure pain. It is not accidental that we use tolerance in relation to pain: tolerance as a moral ideal is directed towards something negative (it would be odd to say, for example, that someone has a high tolerance for pleasure). With this etymology in mind, we can formulate a general definition of toleration that involves three interrelated conditions.[2]

When I tolerate something:

1 I have a negative judgement about this thing (usually a *person or his activities*, where activity is broadly conceived to include the actions, attitudes, and habits of persons).
2 I could negate this thing.
3 I deliberately refrain from negating this thing.

The first condition requires a negative judgement. As I shall explain in the next section, the negative judgement in the case of toleration is not outright disapproval. Rather, let us say that the negative judgements in toleration are midway between approval and outright disapproval; it can be anywhere on a continuum from disgust (at the negative end) to mere non-approving indifference (at the more positive end). The term judgement is used here in a broad sense that includes emotional responses.[3] In general, judgements (including emotions) make discriminations among things and have motivational force. If our judgement of the thing were outright approval, then tolerance would not be needed. Likewise if the judgement were outright disapproval and/or condemnation, then toleration would be impossible. Usually a negative judgement inclines me towards negative action. But tolerance occurs when we resist the negative result of a negative judgement by opposing it with a different judgement.

The second condition states that I have the *power* to express myself negatively towards the thing in question. I use the word *negate* here in a broad sense that allows for a variety of negative reactions, from avoidance to violent destruction.

The third condition states that I *deliberately refrain* from exercising my power to negate the thing. It is important here that I do have power to negate the thing, as in condition 2. I am not tolerant if I go along with something I despise because I am forced to or because I am a coward. In such cases, I lack the power to negate the thing. Rather, I am tolerant when I do not negate the thing I despise even though I could negate it. Instead I endure it or put up with. Finally, my restraint is *deliberate*: I refrain from negating the thing because I have a *reason* not to negate it.

Good reasons for tolerating a thing we could negate are plural and include the following: respect for autonomy; a general commitment to pacifism; concern for other virtues such as kindness and generosity; pedagogical concerns; a desire for reciprocity; a sense of modesty; and others.[4] Each of these provides us with a reason for thinking that toleration is good. This is pointed out because there may be other non-tolerant reasons for refraining from negation: fear, weakness of will, profit motive, etc. Although there are many reasons that toleration is good, I focus in this book primarily on epistemic modesty and respect for autonomy. A sense of our own finitude and fallibility as well as respect for the autonomy of others gives us a good reason to be tolerant.

The complexity and difficulty of toleration

Much has been made about the so-called 'paradox of toleration'.[5] Toleration asks us not to enact the negative consequences of our negative judgements. This becomes paradoxical when we find ourselves confronting persons, attitudes or behaviours that we vigorously reject: we might then, paradoxically, have to tolerate that which we find intolerable. I think that this supposed paradox really misunderstands the range of activities to which toleration applies. If we were asked to tolerate everything including the intolerable (as the paradox suggests), then toleration would be a pernicious idea that would undermine the process of judgement and would, for example, prohibit us from taking steps to prevent atrocities. But we most certainly should reject any moral idea that claims that we should tolerate murder, paedophilia or genocide. Thus we should admit that toleration is for a restricted range of activities, i.e., those that fall short of 'the intolerable'.

We can see this if we consider that there are three categories into which we might place activities.

The three categories of judgement

1 Activities we approve.
2 Activities we do not approve but tolerate.
3 Activities we disapprove and thus find intolerable.

Tolerant people endeavour to keep the second of these categories open, while also making judgements that place certain activities in either category 1 or 3. The basic moral question is exactly where to draw the line between these three categories, especially between categories 2 and 3. I will not answer this question in sufficient detail here, although I assume that those activities we should find intolerable include activities that are gross violations of human rights and would include activities such as murder, paedophilia and genocide. Indeed, we might consider there to be an analytic relationship between the idea of 'the intolerable' and the idea of 'gross violations of human rights'. To flesh out the category of the intolerable would require another book in which human rights are sufficiently defined. For present purposes I simply assume that we do, in general, know what a violation of human rights looks like.

Toleration focuses on those activities of which we do not approve, but which we do not feel compelled to negate. In the previous section I focused on what I called a negative judgement. Thus to refuse to approve something is a negative judgement. But we might think that to not approve of something is actually to disapprove of it, thus placing it in category 3. I want to avoid this bivalent logic and hold out the possibility that there is a range of activities in category 2 that we may view negatively without fully disapproving and pushing these activities into category 3. That which is tolerated is not approved but neither is it disapproved and viewed as intolerable. The difficulty here is that our language and ideas tend to be bivalent. But toleration opens up the possibility of a third category midway between approval and disapproval.

A strictly bivalent view is typical of what might be called fanaticism, where fanaticism is understood to mean the idea that my values are right and all other alternatives are wrong and intolerable. Fanaticism is closely linked to dogmatism. Dogmatism is the assertion of an opinion as true and beyond doubt. Dogmatism is about the logical status of a belief; fanaticism is about the psychological investment that a person has in his beliefs. One of the mistakes that fanatics and dogmatists make is to think in bivalent terms and neglect category 2. Fanatics and dogmatists tend to think 'either you are with me or against me'. Fanatics also tend to think that a person's dignity or worth is found in the ideas or institutions to which he owes allegiance.[6] Tolerance develops when we acknowledge that there are activities that fall in category 2 and that respect for a person can be separated to some extent from judgements about the particular activities of the person.

It should be noted, however, that fanaticism is rare and, I would argue, abnormal because it is rare for an adult to think in completely binary terms. Almost anyone can imagine activities that fall into the category of toleration: activities which are not approved but which are not also disapproved in a more vigorous sense. Nonetheless, it is difficult to make sense of the second category in part because a bivalent view of the world is appealingly simple.

We need good reasons to keep the second category open. Thus far this analysis has described moral psychology from a meta-ethical standpoint, claiming that there are three sorts of moral categories. The problem is that there is no connection between such a descriptive account of moral psychology and the claim that toleration is good. It might be, for example, that we should work to collapse or evacuate the second category – we might think that to judge that activities belong to the second category is to make a mistake or is a sign of self-deception. Thus we need a normative principle or principles that say that it is good for us to be tolerant: principles such as respect for autonomy, acknowledgement of fallibility, an interest in peace, etc. Such normative principles would give us reasons to resist the tendency to slip into the bivalent thinking of the intolerant. Whatever normative principles we use to argue for the value of toleration, it should be noted that one of the results of tolerance is to make moral judgement more complex by preventing us from resorting to simple bivalent thinking.

It is of further use in understanding toleration to draw a distinction between first-order judgements and second-order commitments. At the level of first-order judgements, we find emotional reactions and other practical judgements that focus on concrete activities. These first-order judgements usually occur in a bivalent structure; for example, 'I like it' or 'I don't like it'. At the level of second-order commitments, we find judgements that aim beyond emotion and particularity towards universal principles. Toleration indicates a conflict between a first-order reaction against something and second-order commitment to respect for autonomy or commitment to modesty or self-control. These second-order commitments are supposed to trump first-order reactions. Thus we might have good reasons (based upon our second-order commitments) to refrain from following through on the normal consequences of negative first-order judgements. The philosophical endeavour – from Socrates and the Stoics to the present day – emphasizes the importance of utilizing reason and its second-order commitments to move beyond the merely reactive processes of first-order judgement. Our first-order judgements are emotional responses or immediate perceptions. They are usually bivalent and simplistic. And importantly, they are occasionally false. We have the capacity, as rational beings, to affirm, deny or otherwise criticize our emotional responses and immediate perceptions. Rational beings aim beyond emotional reactions and immediate perceptions towards systematic and self-critical commitments and principles.[7]

This philosophical ideal postulates a norm of human rationality that is difficult to enact. We are usually not nearly as rational as we want to be. We find it difficult to remain committed to our second-order principles because we are deceived by appearances and buffeted by emotion. And we are tempted to succumb to the binary logic of first-order judgement. The difficulty of toleration is related to the tension between first-order reactions and second-order commitments that one finds within one's spiritual economy. Human beings are not simple and transparent entities. Rather, we are complex systems whose parts can conflict. Since Plato, the idea of divisions within the soul has proved useful for analysing conflicts within spiritual life. Plato teaches us that we must struggle to organize our spiritual economy around those second-order principles that he calls the ideas and according to reason, the faculty that knows the ideas. The distinction between first-order reactions and second-order commitments is merely another way of describing such a set of divisions within the soul.

The general challenge of being human is to resolve conflicts within the spiritual economy as best we can. The specific challenge of toleration is that it asks us to restrain some of our most powerful first-order reactions: our negative reactions to persons, attitudes and behaviours. The tension generated by toleration should not be underestimated. Indeed, toleration is only of interest when it results in a general disruption of the spiritual economy. Without such spiritual turmoil, toleration is merely indifference. Indifference usually indicates a failure at the level of first-order judgement: when we are indifferent, we do not have any reaction, negative or positive, to the other. To use the framework generated above, we might say that indifference dissolves all three categories of moral judgement: it avoids approval, disapproval and toleration.

We often confuse indifference with toleration. However, indifference is flawed as a human response for two reasons. First, it rejects the truth of first-order reactions. First-order reactions should not be ignored. Our emotional responses are important ways in which we connect with the world around us. When I react negatively to something, this provides me with important information. While it may turn out that my negative judgement is misinformed or confused, I should not simply reject the process of first-order reaction out of hand by cultivating indifference. Toleration does not ask us to deaden our emotional responses to others; rather it asks us to restrain the negative consequences of our negative emotional responses out of deference to a more universal set of commitments.

Second, indifference is often closely related to general scepticism about moral judgement. The moral sceptic claims that no set of values is true. But sceptical indifference is pernicious or at best amoral. From a moral perspective, clearly some activities should be loved, some should be hated and some should be tolerated. From the perspective of scepticism, both our first-order reactions and our second-order commitments have no objective moral significance. From this scepticism, indifference with regard to moral evaluations may result because all our moral values are thought to be equally groundless. The difficulty here is that moral scepticism cannot lead to the conclusion that it is good to be tolerant, since the sceptic holds that no moral value can be justified. If we claim that toleration is good, it cannot be the same thing as indifference.

This distinction between toleration and indifference is important for explaining the spiritual disruption that occurs with toleration. Indeed, the difficulty of toleration can be understood in terms of the difficulty of the middle path between the sort of indifference in which everything looks the same and the bivalent thinking of the fanatic and dogmatic. Indifference is easy and satisfying because it sets us free, as it were, from the difficult human task of judging. Likewise, intolerance is easy and satisfying because it allows us to rest easy with a primitive sort of binary logic. Toleration is the middle path in which there is a conflict between first-order reaction and second-order commitment; and in which there are more than two sorts of moral judgement. Toleration thus requires self-consciousness and self-control in order to coordinate conflicting parts of the spiritual economy. The discipline required for toleration is part of any idea of education: we must learn to distance ourselves from our first-order reactions in order to move towards universal principles. Our first-order reactions are often misguided or incomplete, in part because they are structured according to the limitations of binary logic. Education does not ask us to reject our first-order reactions, emotional responses or sense perceptions. Rather, it asks us to be self-critical, so that we might remain committed to more important second-order principles.

The difficulty of toleration should not be underestimated. When our brothers and neighbours, friends and countrymen, choose things that we do not like, our emotional reactions can be extreme. We may feel betrayed, lost or alienated. We may feel jealous, envious or resentful. All these emotions are important because they indicate the importance of our relationship with these others who share our lives. We want unity and harmony because we identify ourselves with these others with whom we share so much. This is why we become angry, jealous and resentful. If we did not share so much with these others, perhaps our differences would not bother us so much.[8]

The conclusion, then, is that we need to make our relationships with others more difficult. The easy complaisance of indifference needs to be challenged with a concrete commitment to dialogue and tolerant engagement with the other. The difficulty here is that in recognizing our differences we may find that we had less in common than we thought we had, which is a reason that toleration is linked to tragedy. Although toleration allows for peaceful coexistence with those with whom we disagree, it also admits that there are disagreements that may not be resolvable.

Apathy and relativism

Toleration can become 'heterophilia' or love of difference for its own sake.[9] This can result in a form of postmodern laissez-faire indifference and, indeed, full-blown relativism that is antithetical to communal life and to human flourishing. Michael Walzer has condemned this implication of toleration: 'the postmodern project undercuts every sort of common identity and standard of behavior'.[10] The problem is that a thoroughgoing relativism lacks the resources to combat both anti-democratic political movements and immoral personal behaviour. And it is unable to defend its claims about toleration against its intolerant detractors.

Relativism is a meta-ethical claim about the status of substantive ethical claims. But toleration is a normative principle, not a meta-ethical one. There is no necessary connection between relativism and tolerance.[11] Rather, toleration must be grounded in a substantive moral theory that postulates a set of second-order principles. Unfortunately, we often mistake principles such as a commitment to liberty, impartiality or fairness with a general laissez-faire reluctance to judge others. Such mistakes are understandable. If we are supposed to respect liberty, then it might seem that we are supposed to refrain from judging altogether; indeed, it might seem as if we have no basis upon which to judge others. Michael Sandel expresses this problem in terms of a critique of the sort of relativism he finds typical in certain strands of liberal thought:

> Relativism usually appears less as a claim than as a question: 'Who is to judge?' But the same question can be asked of the values that liberals defend. Toleration and freedom and fairness are values too, and they can hardly be defended by the claim that no values can be defended. So it is a mistake to affirm liberal values by arguing that all values are merely subjective. The relativist defense of liberalism is no defense at all.[12]

Much of this problem results from a confusion about the meaning of key terms. The ideal of impartiality, for example, does not ask us not to judge others. Rather, it asks us to judge everyone (ourselves included) in the same way, according to the same standard. Moreover, liberty does not flourish in an anarchic state. Rather, liberty requires the nurturing of a supportive educational community. Finally, tolerance is not a claim about the relativity of values. Rather, it is a disposition that is based upon some system of values in which tolerance is thought to be good.

Furthermore, apathy and indifference are inimical to tolerance. The apathetic are unwilling to judge because of a lack of passion or commitment. The indifferent are unable to judge because of an inability to differentiate between rival possibilities. The apathetic and the indifferent, then, are not tolerant because the decision to tolerate is a committed response to the other based upon substantive moral commitments. When I tolerate another I decide, for good reasons, not to negate the other. Toleration is not an inability or refusal to judge. Rather, it is a concrete judgement that puts the activities in question into the second category. The indifferent or apathetic *make no decisions* about the category in which an activity belongs; the tolerant *decide* that certain activities are not approved but to be tolerated. Apathy and indifference tend to devolve into a form of disconnection and cynicism that is potentially disastrous for democracy: the apathetic and indifferent undermine or mock our capacity to make substantial decisions, thus preventing us from developing rational discourse about our values.[13]

Apathy, indifference and relativism are antithetical to the development of both a moral self and a moral community. To be a moral self requires passionate commitment to the moral good and a developed capacity for judgement, what Taylor calls 'strong evaluations'.[14] Moral community requires critical interaction among such moral selves. But relativism usually loosens our commitments (although this is not necessarily the case – it is possible to be fanatical about one's own values, while still being committed to a form of meta-ethical relativism). The lack of commitment that results from some forms of relativism may not seem to be a problem, insofar as a loosening of commitment is usually thought to move us away from fanaticism. The problem is, however, that a complete lack of commitment is antithetical to the very idea of moral self-hood. As a movement away from fanaticism, relativism moves too far in the opposite direction. And this poses a further problem insofar as a sincere relativism might find itself unable to criticize fanaticism. If all values are relative, and fanaticism, in whatever form, is a possible value scheme, then the relativist has no way of arguing against the fanatic; indeed, the relativist has no reason not to become fanatical himself.

Moreover, relativism and indifference undermine critical inter-action. If we do not have a firm set of commitments, then it becomes difficult to find grounds for critical engagement with one another. There is no need to criticize you if I am not firmly com-mitted to my own set of values and if I suspect that you are as indif-ferent as I am. Moreover, if relativism is extended deep into the cognitive realm, then it becomes possible that we cannot under-stand one another because of a certain incommensurability or untranslatability between our world-views. But common sense tells us that radical incommensurability is false: most human beings do understand one another about most things.[15] There must be some shared basis in experience that underlies diverse world-views, otherwise relativism risks slipping quickly down the slope towards the sceptical black hole of solipsism.[16] This solipsistic possibility provides another reason to avoid relativ-ism: solipsism can return us to dogmatism. If we cannot understand our basic values, then we have no basis for critical engagement. If this is the case, then we have no reason to listen to one another and we may ironically retreat to our own world-view in a close-minded, dogmatic fashion. In this way, complete relativism, which seems to be the opposite of fanaticism, actually reiterates the same problems found in fanaticism. Fanatics are not interested in critically defending value judgements; relativism supports this idea by telling us that a critical defence of value judgements is impossible.

Some relativists, such as Joseph Margolis, attempt to circum-vent these problems by arguing that the point of relativism is 'that there are no demonstrably valid moral principles' with the intention of throwing the burden of proof back on the defender of absolute values.[17] This book is an attempt to show that the value of tolerance is in fact a good one, although as a falliblist I shy away from the language of absolute value. What I am looking for, then, is the middle ground between dogmatic absolutism and relativism, which I call pluralism. I further want to identify this pluralistic middle ground with the idea of toleration and with the idea of an open-minded inquiry into values.

Pluralism and relativism

One might argue that toleration is something of a condition for the possibility of pluralism: if you are a pluralist, you should be committed to toleration.[18] It is possible that the arrow of implication could be reversed here indicating something of a circle: pluralists should be tolerant and the tolerant should be pluralistic. Pluralists are committed to the idea that many (but not all) different versions of the good have some claim on our moral imaginations. But this indicates a task for moral reflection and dialogue, the precondition of which is toleration: we should tolerate differences as we critically examine ourselves and others while working towards the good and the true. One of the best reasons to be tolerant, then, is that it allows us to work out together whether what we are doing is really one of the plural possibilities for good. This process of 'working out' is the dialogical process that can only occur within a community of tolerant critical interaction.

Pluralism is not relativism.[19] Pluralism holds that there are many ways in which individuals might pursue good. But the pluralist holds that each of these many ways can still be called good, that each is itself a possible manifestation of good. A relativist, by contrast, holds that value is relative to a world-view or conceptual scheme and that there is a problem of translation between conceptual schemes. The difficulty is that if there is no rational mediation between opposed world-views, no way to adjudicate between them, then we are stuck with a struggle for power: a Nietzshean slave-revolt in morality or a Marxist revolution in ideology.

The distinction between relativism and pluralism is slippery. Margolis, for example, complicates things by attempting to speak of a relativist logic (by which he means, in part, a logic that is not bivalent) and by pointing out that radical untranslatability across conceptual schemes of the sort criticized by Donald Davidson is merely one possibility among many – what he calls 'external relativism'. Margolis holds out the hope that his own version of 'internal relativism' possesses the capacity for evaluating competing conceptual schemes. And Margolis strives to distinguish his own relativistic view from pluralism, which he sees as 'simply a doctrine of social tolerance'.[20] Margolis's point is that relativism is a meta-logical doctrine with implications not only for ethics and politics but also for ontology. For Margolis, pluralism is more or less the result of the fact of moral diversity, within some idea of the good that unifies this diversity. Relativism goes farther in claiming that there can be no unifying idea of the good.[21]

Although I am sympathetic to attempts made by Margolis and others to deny unjustified privilege and to resist totalizing points of view that become totalitarian, it seems to me that pluralism, with its commitment to the good – even an as yet undefined good – is better up to the task than relativism. The pluralist need not claim that the idea of the good is already known. Rather, pluralism of the sort that I want to defend treats the idea of 'the good' as an ideal towards which we are struggling as we strive to make sense of our experience of various 'good' objects. We must begin from the Socratic assumption that we do not yet fully know 'the good' even though we talk about all sorts of things as 'good'. This fallibilistic idea is connected with the Socratic command to 'know thyself'. Thus because we are fallible, we should question together the plural goods which we do possess in order to work our way towards mutual understanding about our values. Just as dogmatic absolutism easily becomes despotic in a world inhabited by finite mortal beings, relativism leaves us with that form of apathy and indifference which is the bane of moral development. Moreover, relativism leaves us with no resources with which to combat despotism and fanaticism.[22]

Although we are fallible, we do know some things quite well. Among the things we do know is the fact that we do not know everything. We also know that, with regard to complex questions of value and culture, the justification of knowledge claims often breaks down: often we must act and decide as best we can despite uncertainty. Freedom might then be defined as the right to make mistakes as we struggle to find the good. But the idea that freedom is good is a well-justified claim (and indeed, it can be justified from a variety of perspectives). But there will be a plurality of ways in which freedom can be actualized. If freedom is a good, then this plurality should be allowed. This form of pluralism is not, however, relativism because it begins from the non-relative (although fallible) assumption that freedom is good. Moreover, it will argue (and act) against those who claim that freedom is not a good, i.e., it will be willing to act to negate those who violate the right to be free (even though the very idea of 'right' here can be based upon a plurality of moral theories).

Toward the end of his recent book, *Life Without Principles*, Joseph Margolis points us towards the conclusion that the best we can hope for are 'second-best theories'.[23] He takes this idea from Plato's *Statesman* and uses it to support his resistance to privileged points of view and absolutist theories. This is a useful idea in the struggle against dogmatism. Dogmatists assume that they possess the final theory of the world and they are often willing to implement this theory by force. Anti-dogmatists can at best claim to possess second-best theories. But it is important to note that the idea of a second-best theory need not leave us in the limbo of relativism. Indeed, it is a long way from an absolute theory of the universe to the complete rejection of truth that occurs in the most pernicious forms of relativism. We who live in a second-best universe experience both unity and diversity. We experience diversity but this diversity can be unified in various ways for various purposes. This pluralist point of view follows from recognition of the limits of our imaginations as well as a commitment to transcend these limits as best we can by way of science, philosophy and dialogue.

One way of fleshing out the idea of pluralism is to get a handle on the twin truths that (1) we inhabit a real world of given things and (2) we divide these things up in various ways according to our purposes, i.e., we interpret the world in different ways. In this sense, one can be both a realist and a constructivist.[24] Within limits, it is good to tolerate different interpretations because we can learn more about the world and about ourselves when we are open to different ways of imagining the world. My version of pluralism thus admits variability with regard to our social values; but it also recognizes that some things are simply facts of the matter, which cannot be disputed. This is important because it is then possible for a pluralist to say that some things are false or wrong. Pluralism does not deny that there are standards or criteria of judgement. These standards come from two directions: from the world and from society. Pluralism acknowledges the intersection of these sets of standards; tolerance allows us the space to explore them.

Pluralism and critical toleration

There are standards for behaviour and belief that are set by social conventions and by the world of objective facts. We discover these standards through a variety of experiences including critical dialogue with others. However, a modest recognition of our own fallibility when it comes to judging the activities and beliefs of others will lead us to tolerantly refrain from uncritically negating many of the activities and beliefs which initially appear to us as repugnant. Of course, some activities will be self-negating, some beliefs will be nonsensical and some types of life will be absurd based upon the standards established by physical, biological or social facts. In other words, there are some activities that will fall into category 3 as activities not to be tolerated. A shared world of facts provides the common basis upon which our tolerant, critical interactions can be conducted. However, since judgements are made within a context of meaning, we must endeavour to discover what these contexts are, if we are to criticize one another. This means that we should question and listen carefully to those with whom we disagree, while refraining from carrying out any negative actions implied by our negative judgement. If we judge that beliefs and activities are dangerous to the agent or to others, we ought at the very least to vigorously critique the activity. If it harms others and, in some circumstances, if it harms the agent, then we should intervene. Of course, terms like 'danger' and 'harm' are difficult to define from within a pluralist perspective; but they are not impossible to define – we do share some basic values – which is enough to get the dialogue going.

John Stuart Mill claims that we should not intervene when the activity in question only harms the agent: 'His own good, either physical or moral, is not sufficient warrant [to intervene].'[25] It is possible that activities that we find repugnant are in fact good for people different from ourselves. If such were the case, we might conclude that we ought not intervene. However, it is important to note that the only way we could come to this conclusion would be to engage the other in a dialogue about her activities. One of the best reasons for tolerating the other is because she tells us that she wants to be left alone to pursue her own values. Rather than simply accepting apparently bizarre behaviour we should, then, tolerantly criticize it. As Hans Oberdiek argues: 'Tolerance and vigorous criticism, therefore, go hand in hand.'[26] Critical debate is not opposed to toleration, provided it does not actively negate the behaviour or person criticized. If I care about you as a person, I should both tolerate and positively criticize you. Such tolerant criticism is not negative, i.e., it does not aim at negation.

Rather, it aims at helping the other to make better choices, it works to educate us both, and it serves to foster the development of community by helping us understand one another.

The link between criticism and toleration is easily forgotten in our laissez-faire culture, although it is an essential part of historical discussions of toleration, for example, in both Locke and Mill. Just after Mill claims that we should not intervene for a person's own good he says that, nonetheless, there are 'good reasons for remonstrating with him, or reasoning with him, or persuading him, or entreating him, but not for compelling him, or visiting him with any evil in case he do otherwise'.[27] Locke also recognizes the importance of criticism. After stating that the power of the government is so great that the state ought to be prevented from criticizing its citizens, he states that private citizens need not be so constrained: 'Every man has commission to admonish, exhort, convince another of error, and, by reasoning, to draw him into truth.'[28] For both Locke and Mill, private citizens, who abjure the political power to compel and coerce, are justified in engaging one another in critical moral dialogue. If the reason for toleration is that it is good for us, we should not shy away from other goods including our need for each other's admonishments, exhortations, and criticism – provided of course that these do not become coercive.

Pluralism admits that there are different possible ways to pursue a good life. However, this does not mean that all life-choices are equally good – it is always possible to become better. Our interest in the good requires that we criticize one another tolerantly with the spirit of modesty that is typical of that type of education that acknowledges human finitude and fallibility. The sort of non-interference and non-criticism that might be called laissez-faire indifference fits better with moral relativism than with moral pluralism. Relativists explicitly deny that criticism across difference can be intelligible. In this sense relativism expresses a type of hubris that runs counter to the spirit of modesty that is characteristic of tolerant moral criticism. Since Socrates, philosophers have argued that we should recognize the limits of our capacity to judge the good both for ourselves and for others. But these limits are only discovered by way of social criticism, deliberation and education. Tolerance is a virtue that makes possible pluralistic debate about the good life. Relativism allows no such debate because it cannot even guarantee that the terms of discourse are equally meaningful for each of the participants, nor can it claim that dialogue is good. Pluralism maintains, on the contrary, that criticism and education are part of any good life for human beings. Although there are many ways that dialogue may be engaged and many conclusions that can be reached, these plural possibilities do not undermine the claim that tolerant dialogue is good for human beings.

Notes

1. See Preston King, *Toleration*, 2nd edition, London: Frank Cass, 1998, p. 12 or Hans Oberdiek, *Tolerance: Between Forbearance and Acceptance*, Lanham, MD: Rowman and Littlefield, 2001, chapter 6.

2. A similar threefold structure is described by Glen Newey in *Virtue, Reason, and Toleration*, Edinburgh: University of Edinburgh Press, 1999, p. 73. Also see Geoffrey Harrison, 'Relativism and Tolerance' in Michael Krausz and Jack W. Meiland (eds) *Relativism: Cognitive and Moral*, Notre Dame, IN: University of Notre Dame Press.

3. On this basically Stoic conception of emotion as judgement see Martha Nussbaum, *The Therapy of Desire*, Princeton, NJ: Princeton University Press, 1994, p. 366–86; also Nussbaum, *Upheavals of Thought*, Cambridge: Cambridge University Press, 2001, chapter 1.

4. This pluralist approach is similar to Bernard Williams' conclusions in 'Toleration: A Political or Moral Question' in Paul Ricouer (ed.) *Tolerance Between Intolerance and the Intolerable* (this is an edition of *Diogenes*) no. 176, vol. 44/4, Winter, 1996, p. 47.

5. Karl Popper names the paradox in *The Open Society and its Enemies*, Princeton, NJ: Princeton University Press, 1971, I: 265, note 4; also cf. Popper, 'Toleration and Intellectual Responsibility' in Susan Mendus and David Edwards (eds), *On Toleration*, Oxford: Clarendon Press, 1987. Further discussion of the paradox of toleration can be found in

Bernard Williams, 'Toleration: An Impossible Virtue' in David Heyd (ed.) *Toleration: An Elusive Virtue*, Princeton, NJ: Princeton University Press, 1996.

6. Francis Fukuyama links fanaticism to the drive for recognition in *The End of History and the Last Man*, New York: The Free Press, 1992, p. 214.

7. See Nussbaum *Upheavals of Thought*, chapter 1.

8. Michael Ignatieff has argued that toleration is most difficult (and intolerance most violent) when it is directed towards those with whom we share the most in common in 'Nationalism and Toleration' in Susan Mendus (ed.) *The Politics of Toleration in Modern Life*, Durham, NC: Duke University Press, 2000.

9. I borrow 'heterophilia' from Zygmunt Baumann, *Postmodernity and Its Discontents*, New York: New York University Press, 1997.

10. Michael Walzer, *On Toleration*, New Haven, CT: Yale University Press, 1999, p. 88.

11. See Hye-Kyung Kim and Michael Wreen in 'Relativism, Absolutism, and Tolerance' in *Metaphilosophy*, 34:4 (July 2003), 447–59; also see John W. Cook, *Morality and Cultural Differences*, Oxford: Oxford University Press, 1999, especially pp. 26–9.

12. Michael Sandel, *Democracy's Discontent*, Cambridge, MA: Harvard University Press, 1996, p. 8. For an explicit response to this sort of critique see Will Kymlicka, *Liberalism, Community, and Culture*, Oxford: Clarendon Press, 1989, pp. 9–10.

13. See Robert Bellah *et al.*, *Habits of the Heart*, Berkeley, CA: University of California Press, 1996; also see Jean Bethke Elshtain, *Democracy on Trial*, New York: Basic Books, 1995.

14. Charles Taylor, *Sources of the Self*, Cambridge, MA: Harvard University Press, 1989, chapter 2; also see Charles Taylor, 'The Person' in Carrithers, Collins and Lukes (eds) *The Category of the Person*, Cambridge: Cambridge University Press, 1985.

15. Donald Davidson has shown the limits of such a radical cognitive relativism in his 'On the Very Idea of a Conceptual Scheme' in Michael Krausz and Jack W. Meiland (eds), *Relativism: Cognitive and Moral*, Notre Dame, IN: University of Notre Dame Press, 1982.

16. See Louis Pojman, 'Who's to Judge' in Christina Summers and Fred Sommers (eds), *Vice and Virtue in Everyday Life* 5th edition, Fort Worth, TX: Harcourt College Publishers, 2001.

17. Joseph Margolis, *Life Without Principles*, Cambridge, MA: Blackwell, 1996, p. 201.

18. On the use of transcendental arguments in the context of pluralism and falliblism see Sami Pihlström, *Naturalizing the Transcendental*, New York: Humanity Books, 2003, especially chapter 7, for the application to ethics.

19. For a useful discussion see John Kekes, *Pluralism in Philosophy: Changing the Subject*, Ithaca, NY: Cornell University Press, 2000.

20. Joseph Margolis, *Pragmatism Without Foundations*, Oxford: Basil Blackwell, 1986, p. 54.

21. Joseph Margolis, *Life Without Principles*, Cambridge, MA: Blackwell, 1996, p. 105; also John Kekes, *Pluralism in Philosophy*, p. 78.

22. For more on relativism vs. falliblism see Karl Popper, 'Toleration and Intellectual Responsibility' in Mendus and Edward (eds) *On Toleration*, pp. 25–6.

23. Joseph Margolis, *Life Without Principles*, epilogue.

24. For a useful discussion of realism vs. constructivism see Michael Krausz, *The Limits of Rightness*, Lanham, MD: Rowman and Littlefield, 2000; for a pragmatic account see Sami Pihlström, *Naturalizing the Transcendental*.

25. John Stuart Mill, *On Liberty*, Oxford: Oxford World Classics, 1998, p. 14.

26. Hans Oberdiek, *Tolerance*, p. 149.

27. Mill, *On Liberty*, p. 14.

28. John Locke, *Letter Concerning Toleration* in Steven M. Cahn (ed.) *Classics of Political and Moral Philosophy*, New York: Oxford University Press, 2002, p. 295.

3

Tolerance, Modesty and the Limits of the Moral Imagination

I have argued that there are plural reasons to be tolerant. These reasons include a commitment to pacifism, a desire for reciprocity, pedagogical self-restraint, respect for autonomy and modesty. Here I will focus on the last of these and will argue that tolerance can and should be developed from a modest admission of finitude and fallibility. I understand modesty to be the opposite of pride, irascibility and the tendency to abuse power, all of which can be included in the idea of *hubris*. Modesty is linked to Aristotelian virtues such as self-control or continence (*enkrates*), moderation or temperance (*sophrosyne*), and fairness or clemency (*epieikeia*). Aristotle discusses something like modesty under the heading 'mildness' (*praotēs*) and in connection with considerateness or for-givingness (*sungnōmē*).[1] A Greek term that comes close to what I have in mind is *aidos*, which can be translated as 'shame', 'modesty', 'sense of honor', or 'propriety'.[2]

Modesty has not been without its detractors. On the one hand, modesty may be confused with humility and thus linked to a sort of grovelling self-abnegation. Or modesty may be thought to be a sort of false social nicety: a mere appearance of non-self-assertion. Spinoza disparages modesty in this way: 'Politeness or modesty (*humanitas seu modestia*) is the desire of doing such things as please men and omitting such as do not.'[3] The problem with Spinoza's definition is that it turns toleration and modesty into a desire to please, which is not what I have in mind here. Rather, I argue that modesty follows from an honest appraisal of one's fallibility and finitude.[4] The sort of modesty I have in mind is not the same as self-abnegation or humiliation. Rather, modesty results from a serious appraisal of the limits of one's power of judgement. It inclines one to restrain oneself from following through on first-order judgements, out of recognition of the possibility that these judgements may be mistaken.

Since we often fail to fully imagine the circumstances of the others with whom we interact, we should be cautious in acting upon our negative judgements. This is not a new argument. Indeed, it connects back to Socrates and to a general idea of moderation in judgement and action. In the sixteenth century, Montaigne indicated: 'it is ordinary to see good intentions, if they are carried out without moderation, push men to very vicious acts'.[5] In the eighteenth century Voltaire linked modesty more explicitly to tolerance: 'What is tolerance? It is the consequence of humanity. We are all formed of frailty and error; let us pardon reciprocally each other's follies – that is the first law of nature.' He concludes: 'It is clearer still that we ought to be tolerant of one another, because we are all weak, inconsistent, liable to fickleness and error.'[6]

Usually, the moral ideal of tolerance is developed from within an ethic, such as Millian liberalism, which respects the autonomy of individuals. From this perspective one restrains oneself out of deference to the higher value of autonomy. This approach is crucial, especially in the realm of political toleration. However, a focus on modesty allows us to see the link between tolerance and criticism in the pursuit of a philosophical community. My claim is that tolerance can and should be developed from self-conscious recognition of the limits of the moral imagination. When we follow the twin philosophical commands, 'know thyself' and 'nothing in excess', we can become tolerant and can begin to construct a fragile community of enquiry in which we work together to understand ourselves. Since our capacity to imagine the total situation of the other is limited, we should be cautious in judging others and thus should tend towards tolerance. Modest recognition of our limits need not lead to inaction and passivity, even though tolerance implies a certain open-minded and falliblist approach.

I will approach modesty and tolerance by focusing on the limits of imagination. Modesty asks us to consider whether we are able to imagine the circumstances and experience of the other. Toleration results when I imagine that the other's actions are autonomous, even while recognizing that I cannot imagine all the values that lead the other to act in the way she does. And so imaginative connection is required for tolerance, as is recognition of the limits of the imagination. Such a dialectic of imagination is crucial for the creation of dialogical community. On the one hand, the imagination must expand to take in the situation of the other in order to understand and judge the other. On the other hand, the imagination must limit itself out of a self-conscious recognition of its inability fully to take in the situation of the other. The first side of this dialectic accounts for the possibility of criticism and dialogue; the second side describes the need for self-criticism, modesty and tolerance. Together they explain the tragedy of communities built on tolerance: tolerance is required when we acknowledge the possible failure of the imagination.

A totalizing judgement – whether positive or negative – requires us to assume that we have expanded our imaginations enough to take in the total situation of the other. But our ability to make such totalizing judgements is limited. It is useful to remind ourselves – following, for example, Nietzsche – that many of our attitudes towards others can be disguises for will to power: compassion and condemnation can both disguise a desire for superiority. Moreover, since attitudes and behaviours occur within complex situations, we must be cautious when we attempt to comprehend the experience of the other. We are often tempted to believe that we can imagine the experience of an other. This hope often occurs out of a sincere desire for solidarity and mutual respect. However, one must be careful that the desire for solidarity does not express itself in a monological voice, which conceals either will to power or ignorance.

The promise of the imagination: David Norton and Martin Buber

Imagination is necessary for a variety of human activities in which we must expand our perspective: in understanding stories, translating foreign languages, writing ethnographies and, indeed, in the process of education itself.[7] This idea is found in the recent work of David Norton, who derives it from Martin Buber. Buber claims that imagination is the basis for interpersonal relationships: 'Applied to intercourse between men, imagining the real means that I imagine to myself what another man is at this very moment wishing, feeling, perceiving, thinking, and not as a detached content but in his very reality, that is, as a living process in this man.'[8] Buber's point is that concrete human interaction requires us to imagine the reality experienced by the other. Norton argues that this productive expansion of perspectives grounds the virtue that he calls *liberality* (which seems to include respect, generosity, sympathy and compassion). Norton writes: 'By the virtue of "liberality" I refer to the cultivated disposition to recognize and appreciate truths and values other than one's own ... Where others' truths and values are incommensurable with our own, recognition and appreciation of them as the truths and values they represent require that we lend ourselves to the viewpoint of those whose truths and values they are – we exchange our perspectival world for theirs – by the exercise of transcendental imagination.'[9]

Norton's idea draws upon the common idea of 'putting oneself in the place of the other' or 'walking in someone else's shoes'. If we could do this, we would have sympathy for the other, and although we might disagree with the other we could 'understand where he was coming from'. The further point is that if one is to make a legitimate critique of the other, one must understand the context of meaning in which her beliefs or activities occur. For critique to get off the ground it must be possible to imaginatively adopt a position internal to the other's perspective.

This is what Buber has in mind when he talks about 'genuine dialogue'. A genuine dialogue is one in which the partners turn towards each other with respect such that each is there in the dialogue as a whole: each is a Thou to the other's I – 'But the speaker does not merely perceive the one who is present to him in this way; he receives him as his partner, and that means that he confirms this other being, so far as it is for him to confirm.'[10] Of course, Buber recognizes that this dialogical situation is not an easy one. Rather, the most 'fruitful' of genuine dialogues seem to skirt the edge of destruction because of the basic ambiguity of language, thought and experience: 'It is not the unambiguity of a word but its ambiguity that constitutes living language. The ambiguity creates the problematic of speech, and it creates its overcoming in an understanding that is not an assimilation but a fruitfulness.'[11] Misunderstandings and differences that result from the ambiguity of words, thoughts and experience show us the need for dialogue. The ambiguity of our experience (our differences and misunderstandings) is what leads us into dialogue in the first place. Imagination is the faculty that allows us to engage one another in fruitful dialogue despite our differences.

These discussions point beyond toleration towards something stronger, perhaps what might be called respect or recognition. Hegel's discussion of recognition and the master–slave dialectic has influenced contemporary discussions of multiculturalism.[12] With regard to the issue of multiculturalism, Amy Gutmann notes that 'toleration extends to the widest range of views, so long as they stop short of threats and other direct and discernible harms to individuals. Respect is far more discriminating.'[13] The idea behind this distinction is that toleration is passive and negative while respect aims more positively at recognizing the legitimacy of moral difference by way of discourse and debate: 'mutual respect requires a widespread willingness and ability to articulate our disagreements, to defend them before people with whom we disagree'.[14] I agree that mutual critical interaction and respect are important for human beings. However, the idea of respect is too positive in some cases. Respect assumes that we know before hand that the other's values are worthy of consideration and debate. But often we lack such assurance. Thus toleration remains essential in many social situations. Moreover, toleration can be linked with that sort of critical engagement with the other that Gutmann sees as the basis of respect.

One of the problems for toleration is arrogance, especially understood as a sort of un-self-conscious ethnocentrism. Charles Taylor notes that 'arrogance' often precludes us from being open to others.[15] We must admit our own limitations – including our tendency towards hubris and ethnocentrism – when we find ourselves engaged with others whom we do not properly understand. Norton's ideal of liberality and Gutmann's idea of respect are perhaps too much to ask of us. Respect appears to make a judgement that puts the activities of the other into the first category discussed in Chapter 2: respect seems to be a form of approval. But tolerance is for activities that we do not approve. If we modestly admit our own fallibility, then we must admit that we do not yet have the resources fully to imagine the other or fully to respect them, which is why we need the second category discussed in Chapter 2 and why we cannot reduce all judgements to approval or disapproval. If I cannot fully imagine her circumstances, it will be difficult to decide whether to approve or disapprove of the other's activities. This issue is especially pressing with regard to questions of multiculturalism, where we suspect that we lack adequate understanding of the contexts of alien cultures. The best we can do is admit our limits, while allowing for the possibility of the second category of judgement, while working to learn more about the other so that we might make better judgements.

The failure of the imagination

Although I am sympathetic to the hope that we can expand our horizons to include the perspective of the other, we must be careful to admit our frequent failure to imagine the perspective of the other. We see this lack of imagination in personal and professional relationships as well as in the larger struggles of history. Of course, here I am making an empirical generalization to which it will be easy to come up with counter-examples. I am *not* arguing that it is *impossible* to get inside the mind or world of the other. Indeed, I am sure that Buber's genuine dialogues do occasionally happen. Rather, I am arguing that as a matter of fact we often fail to imagine the perspective of the other. In light of the ubiquity of this failure, tolerance is an important virtue.

Failures of imagination can be divided into two categories: intrapersonal failures and interpersonal failures. It is important to recognize the possibility of the first because, as we shall see, self-knowledge is presupposed for those more robust dialogical communities towards which we would like to develop.

Intrapersonal failures

Most of us fail to understand ourselves. One concrete example of this is the fact that we often fail to imagine what our own future interests might be. This is not a problem of a lack of prudence. Nor is it like Parfit's discussion of a 'bias towards the present' when we weigh our present interests against our future interests.[16] Rather, we often find it difficult, if not impossible, to imagine what our interests will be at a future time.

An obvious example is sex. Children are unable to imagine what their own future interest in sex will be. In the same way, adolescents and young adults are unable to imagine what their interest in sex will be in their old age. This problem can be grounded in certain biological changes – most obviously the development of sexuality during puberty and its eventual senescence. Metaphorically speaking, the caterpillar cannot fully imagine what it will be like to be a butterfly. But the problem can also be grounded in cultural reinterpretations. Thus the event of rape, a promise made in marriage, or a religious conversion can all change the very experience of sex in a way that can not be fully imagined until the change occurs. Gandhi's conversion to *brahmacharya* or Augustine's conversion to continence provide concrete examples. When Augustine and Gandhi were finally converted and renounced sexual pleasure, the experience of sexuality was itself transformed in a way that could not be fully imagined before taking the vow of celibacy.[17] Such a transformation is difficult to imagine for one who has not yet gone through this transformation. And this is precisely the problem: we have difficulty imagining situations of which we have no experience and to which we have not yet committed ourselves. Although we can utilize analogies, these analogies are often weak. (For example, 'giving up sex is like giving up smoking'.) This difficulty stems from the fact that our experiences of even basic bodily functions are replete with meaning: the meaning of sex is quite different from the meaning of smoking. And the meaning of these activities can be radically transformed even within the course of our own lives.

Interpersonal failures

Given the fact that we can fail to imagine what our own future experiences might be like, it is even more likely that we can fail to imagine what another person's experience is like. Indeed, we often fail to imagine the experiences of our most intimate companions. We see this failure daily in the minor miscommunications that infect our personal and professional lives. Although it is perhaps possible to imagine the total situation of another, this is a very difficult task. At this point I am going to paint an admittedly extreme picture of these difficulties, recognizing that occasionally we are able to imagine the situation of the other. Gender difference provides a ubiquitous example. Even though my wife and I have shared our lives together for more than a decade, she is still mysterious to me. I cannot imagine what it is to be a woman in either a biological or cultural sense. I cannot imagine, for example, what her experience of childbirth or her experience of breastfeeding was like. Nor can I imagine her daily experience of the subtle (and not so subtle) forms of sexism that still persist in our society. I can utilize analogies here, but these analogies are usually quite lame. Concrete differences in life experience always make interpersonal relationships a challenge, including differences in gender, age, race, body shape and ability, class, education, language, religion and other cultural differences. The number of important differences cannot be underestimated.

Tolerance and condemnation: suicide and sati

I have suggested that we should tolerate when we are unable fully to imagine the situation of the other. However, although lack of understanding provides us with a reason to tolerate the other and his activities, we must act upon our best judgement (in light of self-consciousness about our own ignorance), when we encounter activities that demand a response, such as intolerable activities that violate human rights. These responses will vary in light of the circumstances. However, the rule of thumb we should adopt, following Mill, is that we can only consider toleration when there is no harm done to others. Harm to others is the limit of toleration. The idea of rights establishes certain immunities from harm. We should not tolerate activities in which one individual violates the rights of another. Toleration seems most suitable for self-regarding activities in which individuals, if they harm anyone, seem only to harm themselves. This is true because the individual herself is usually assumed to be the best judge of what is harmful to her. Of course, there are problems with this idea such as the problem of ideology and the possibility of self-deception. But the basic idea is that it is difficult to judge what is harmful or good for the other because we often cannot imagine her concrete situation. Despite this, there are limits to what we should tolerate, even from this point of view. The limits of toleration can be found in the question of whether we can imagine that the other's actions are in fact autonomous. I will discuss two related examples: suicide and sati.

Example 1: suicide

I find being alive to be a good thing. Although I have experienced difficulties and despair, I find it hard to imagine ever seriously contemplating suicide. I have read novels and poems and have seen films about suicide. I have talked with people who have attempted suicide. Nonetheless, it is hard to imagine that the suicide is making the right decision. Indeed, in most cases I believe that the suicide is making the wrong decision and that he needs medication or therapy. However, I can imagine not wanting to live in the case of a debilitating illness or even in the case of great despair or a monumental loss of honour, or some other circumstance. This glimmer of imaginative identification allows me to believe that it might be possible that for someone else, suicide might be the right choice. And since suicide causes no direct harm to others (I realize that this is debatable), I am inclined to tolerate suicide. This does not mean that I will be indifferent to the suicide. Indeed, it is my moral obligation to help the suicide to find a reason to live. Thus I will argue, exhort, admonish and seek to inspire the other. However, I will allow the suicide to go through with her actions because, in fact, I admit that I cannot fully imagine the despair or suffering that the other is experiencing just as I cannot imagine the relief that this person would find in death.

Even if we bring religion into consideration here, the same sorts of arguments hold. One might object that certain religions clearly state that suicide is wrong. The religious view may give me further reasons to exhort and admonish; indeed, it may give me further arguments to use as I try to convince the potential suicide not to go through with his intentions. But unless it can be shown that the potential suicide will substantially harm others or violate the rights of others in palpable ways, I believe we must allow the person to kill himself. From a tolerant religious perspective, I have to admit at a certain point that the individual's relation to God is up to him. Even though I might use religious arguments to persuade the other, I should not, ultimately, prevent him from making choices that contravene religious teaching, unless it is clear that these choices will harm others.

Example 2: sati

When we take up issues of intercultural communication, the difficulties of imaginative connection with the other become extreme. I frankly find myself at a loss to imagine what it would be like to be a Hindu widow who is ready to immolate herself on her dead husband's funeral pyre. This is not a suicide of despair but, rather, voluntary self-incineration in pursuit of beatification.[18] It is important to note here that when discussing the example of sati, an interpretation of it that states that it is voluntary is itself subject to dispute.[19] For me, it is difficult to imagine that this act might be autonomous, although I admit that the pre-immolation ritual of burning fingers or hands, which is often a part of sati, seems to indicate a willingness to burn. Nonetheless, I can only imagine that the Hindu widow is coerced by a patriarchal society to such an extent that she has no choice but to go along with the ritual. Indeed, there has been debate about the interpretation of the acts of the widow during the immolation. Where sati defenders see the widow waving in blessing from the burning pyre, anti-sati witnesses see the widow quaking in pain and protest.

I might begin to expand my imagination here by focusing on certain basic facts that seem ubiquitous to all persons. Both the widow and I eat, drink and sleep. We both think according to certain logical rules. We both have views about self and world. We are both concerned with family and with death. My imagination might focus on what is common to us as mortal, rational, biological organisms. This soft universalism does make the imaginative task easier. We all have bodies, we all have family ties, we all possess language and culture, we all confront death and we are concerned with the ultimate destination of our souls. Anyone who has visited a foreign culture can attest to the fact that certain shared features of our humanity do exist and make possible interpersonal and intercultural communication

But this imaginative connection seems too thin to account for the difference, which separates me from the Hindu widow. Based upon analogy with my own experience and with my limited knowledge of her religion, I can certainly explain the ideas and world-views, which lead her to want to commit this act. She understands her own life within the context of a patriarchal religion in which the mortal body (especially of a woman) is transient and insignificant. Indeed, she will be celebrated as a saint after her death. I *can imagine* wanting to be deified in this way: it is possible to imagine the desire for beatification. The problem is that I *cannot imagine* myself into a situation in which I would actually believe that burning myself alive on my husband's funeral pyre would result in beatification. I cannot make the conversion necessary for full understanding, although my imagination can come up with all sorts of analogies. I might imagine that sati is related to the suicide of despair discussed above, or to our death rituals or to our processes of mourning. But sati is not despair or mourning. Rather, it is a religious exaltation of wifely devotion. I might imagine that sati is like sacrificing oneself for the good of one's family, for example, rushing into the burning house to save one's children. But sati is not utilitarian in this way. Rather it is an act of religious consummation in which the self is sacrificed out of duty without any positive consequence in this world. Thus my imagination fails to connect me to the actual thoughts and beliefs and the concrete world-view of sati. And although this case is extreme, the problem is that I bring my own feet with me, as it were, whenever I step into another's shoes.

Tolerance and action

With regard to sati, I find not only that I cannot imagine the state of mind of the widow but also that I cannot imagine that such an act would really be autonomous. I suspect coercion and manipulation seen in the public nature of the ritual, in the young age of the usual sati widow and in the supporting role played by other members of the community (who are usually – but not always – men). Moreover, I doubt the religious claims that support it. And so I support those Indian laws that prohibit it and I am inclined to criticize a religion that celebrates sati and to argue that such a religion is misogynistic and inhumane. After all, we must judge and act as best we can, even in the light of the sorts of philosophical questions I am raising here about our capacity to judge. When one *must act* in this way when confronted with a practice such as sati, one must focus on the question of burden of proof. One must judge based upon the preponderance of evidence. Most of the evidence I have examined points to the wrongness of sati. It is up to the proponent of sati to prove that sati is not misogynistic, inhumane and immoral. Nonetheless, if we recognize the sorts of considerations I am discussing here, we must retain an open mind and pursue continued critical dialogue with the proponent of sati. If it could be established that sati were truly a voluntary act of suicide, understandable on analogy with those sorts of suicide that I am inclined to tolerate, I would be inclined to tolerate it as well.

I realize that I might be ethnocentric in my condemnation of sati. A tolerant approach must self-critically recognize the continuing possibility of ethnocentrism, while refusing to shy away from condemning an action, belief or culture that, on the face of it, is wrong. After all, occasionally we must judge and act to prevent evil. But tolerance asks us to recognize our own fallibility and need for education, dialogue and self-criticism. Thus it may be possible to condemn an activity (and place it in the third category) in a tolerant spirit that is open to education and revision.

Continued dialogue is important because I must admit that if my imagination fails me, I cannot be sure that I have fully understood what I am condemning. I find that I need more education to help me develop my imaginative capacities so that I might begin to form a basis of interpersonal experience such that I might be willing to tolerate sati. The connections found in the soft universals that we all share are insufficient here. Rather than vague generalizations about universal human nature, I need concrete particulars if my imagination is going to function properly. Nonetheless, I can remain tolerant, even in condemning sati, if I am willing to keep my mind open to further education and the possible expansion of my imagination.

Perhaps, then, Norton's idea of liberality is too much to ask of finite creatures with limited experience and failing imaginations. Rather than asking us to perform the extraordinary feat of 'exchanging our perspectival world for theirs' in an act of liberality that would go, in Norton's words, 'beyond tolerance', perhaps the best we can do is ask one another to be tolerant until such a time as we have enough concrete experience upon which to base our imaginative activity.[20] We must remain tolerant because we are often unable to imagine fully the experience of the other. If we have admitted that our imaginative ability often fails, then we must further admit that our ability to judge others is limited. Thus tolerance is the proper disposition for a person who realizes his or her own failures of imagination. Of course, this does not mean that we cannot act, that we cannot criticize and that we cannot prohibit seemingly harmful actions. Rather, it means that even in criticizing and prohibiting these sorts of activities, we must admit our own fallibility and continually seek to foster tolerant, yet critical, dialogue.

Tolerance and ignorance

The argument that I have been making assumes that we are, at least in part, mysteries to each other and to ourselves. I shall develop this idea in subsequent chapters.[21] The biggest problem here is that our lack of self-knowledge limits our ability to judge others (both to sympathize with them and to condemn them) because we find that we lack the basis for judgement. Self-knowledge is the basis for judging the other because, as adumbrated above, our imaginative identification with the other is based upon certain analogies with the self. I imagine celibacy by way of analogy with giving up smoking. I imagine my wife's experience of childbirth by way of other admittedly lame analogies. I imagine the Hindu widow's experience by way of an analogy with those soft universals that connect us insofar as I understand them in myself. But, it is important to remember that analogical reasoning is limited, especially when we are not sure of the meaning of the object of comparison. In general the object of comparison in these cases is myself – my own experiences. If I still do not understand myself and my own experiences, then I find my analogical reasoning to be even more suspect.

There are two ways that this argument might go: a strong version and a weak version.

1 The strong version. One might argue that if we are to begin to criticize others, we must first possess self-knowledge. From this

point of view, if we do not have self-knowledge, then we cannot
begin to criticize others. (This follows from *modus tollens*.)

2   The weak version. One might argue, more moderately, that if
    we possess self-knowledge, then we have a basis from which to
    criticize others. From this point of view, if we do not have self-
    knowledge, nothing necessarily follows. (Otherwise we would
    commit the fallacy of denying the antecedent.)

Said differently, the strong version claims that if there is no
self-knowledge, then there can be no criticism of others. The weak
version says that if there is no self-knowledge, then our basis
for criticism must be shifted to some other ground. We might be
reluctant to fully adopt the strong version because of a resistance
to fully placing the ground of criticism on self-knowledge. I am
sympathetic to the strong version, however, because it does seem
that self-knowledge is required before we are to begin criticizing
others. At any rate, if we accept the premise of the weak version
and if we accept that we do not have self-knowledge, then we
must find some other ground for criticism. Some suggestions for
this other ground include: knowledge of God or knowledge
of human nature. We might then claim, for example, that if we
have knowledge of the essence of human nature, then we have a
ground for criticizing others (and indeed for criticizing ourselves).

The problem – and the reason I am sympathetic to the strong
version – is that knowledge of human nature itself seems to
require self-knowledge. The philosophical question must be:
'How do I know that *my knowledge* of human nature is authorita-
tive?' With this question, I am thrown back upon the problem of
self-knowledge (as seen in Socrates, Descartes or Kant to name a
few): if I am not even sure who or what I am, I cannot justify my
claims about the essence of human nature. So the 'other ground'
for criticism espoused in the weak version itself devolves back to
self-knowledge. More concretely, we might assume that the soft
universals assumed in cross-cultural dialogue are some sort of

natural fact, which we can then utilize to understand the other. However, these soft universals are themselves quite mysterious. For example, sati is a death ritual. But what is the significance of death rituals? All cultures have them, but why do we have them and what is their significance? More basically, what is the meaning of the death rituals in our own culture? Unless I fully understand my own need for and practice of death rituals, and my own culture's understanding of martyrdom and transience, I will have a hard time imagining sati.

It thus seems that the premise of the strong version ought to be maintained: 'we can criticize others only if we possess self-knowledge'. Connecting this back to Norton's idea of liberality and imagination, we can conclude that we can respect, sympathize and/or condemn others only to the extent that we are able to understand ourselves. However, if we do not possess self-knowledge, i.e., if we are mysteries to ourselves, then our comportment to others should be tolerant.

Conclusion: tolerance and education

The irony here is that one must have a self-knowledge in order to recognize one's own failures of imagination. Thus tolerance is the result of philosophical education. Education towards tolerance must begin from our innate trust in our own imaginative capacities. Normal children possess rich imaginative faculties and the capacity for analogical thinking. Good education takes advantage of this capacity by expanding the experience of self and world in multiple directions by the study of literature, history, art, etc. In this way we lead children beyond ethnocentrism and closed-mindedness as we help them imagine alternative world-views. However, in order to avoid the Nietzchean pitfall indicated at the outset of this chapter – where imagination masks will to power – this process of imaginative expansion should be accompanied by philosophical self-consciousness of the limits of our imaginations.

Otherwise ethnocentrism is simply reiterated at a higher level. This occurs when we say, for example, 'celibacy is just like giving up smoking' or 'sati is just like a Christian funeral'. Rather than making these banal (in Arendt's sense, which she links to the inability to 'think from the standpoint of somebody else') and unimaginative comparisons, we should learn to recognize the fact that often we cannot fully imagine the experience of the other.[22] Thus, even when we must judge others, perhaps we can remain tolerant.

Finally, it is through this self-conscious restraint of imagination that we can begin to move towards that more critical dialogical encounter with the other that Buber called 'genuine meeting'. Buber's hope is that in such meetings 'man learns not merely that he is limited by man, cast upon his own finitude, partialness, need of completion, but his own relation to truth is heightened by the other's different relation to the same truth – different in accordance with his individuation, and destined to take seed and grow differently'.[23] One of the precursors of genuine dialogue is that form of tolerant self-restraint that occurs out of recognition of our own limited capacity to imagine the experience of the other. We only learn to listen to the other after we have learned to deliberately restrain our judging faculties in light of a developed sense of the limits of imagination. But tolerance does not have to leave us indifferent to one another, unable to communicate, each of us confined in a solipsistic scepticism. While we might want *political* entities to be tolerantly indifferent in this way, such indifference and apathy do not form part of a good life for human beings. Tolerance at the level of interaction among individuals develops out of self-consciousness about our native desire to imagine the experience of the other to communicate with the other and, yes, to judge the other. We must cultivate this innate drive of the imagination while recognizing its limits. We must not be afraid of judging others because we cannot remain indifferent in the face of suffering and injustice. And yet we must recognize the inherent limits of the judging faculty. Tolerance is a proper restraint upon the irrepressible imagination, which recognizes that the imagination tends to fill in the gaps with fanciful ideas and banal comparisons. Indeed, such unbridled use of the imagination often results in intolerant fanaticism: as we begin to imagine the other as an alien who must be destroyed. Tolerance resists this fantastic and often fanatical work of the imagination with the realistic recognition that often gaps remain. While the imagination makes possible critical interaction with the other, self-criticism and tolerance prevent this critical interaction from becoming dogmatic and, in fact, unimaginative.

Notes

1. Aristotle, *Nicomachean Ethics*, p. 1125b.
2. See Douglas L. Cairns, *Aidos: The Psychology and Ethics of Honor and Shame in Ancient Greek Literature*, Oxford: Clarendon Press, 1993.
3. Spinoza, *Ethics*, Third Part, Definition 43, trans. Andrew Boyle, London: J.M Dent Orion Publishing, 1993, p. 136.
4. Cf. Norberto Bobbio, 'In Praise of *La Mitezza*' in Paul Ricouer (ed.) *Tolerance Between Intolerance and the Intolerable* (this is an edition of *Diogenes*), No. 176, Vol. 44/4, Winter, 1996.
5. Montaigne, 'Of Freedom of Conscience' in *Essays*, trans. Donald M. Frame, Stanford, CA: Stanford University Press, 1958, p. 506. See Alan Levine, *Sensual Philosophy: Toleration, Skepticism, and Montaigne's Politics of the Self*, Lanham, MD: Lexington Books, 2001.
6. Voltaire, *Philosophical Dictionary*, Cleveland, OH: World Publishing Co., 1943, pp. 302, 304. Popper discusses Voltaire in Karl Popper, 'Toleration and Intellectual Responsibility' in Susan Mendus and David Edwards (eds), *On Toleration*, Oxford: Clarendon Press, 1987, p. 18.
7. David Norton, *Imagination, Understanding, and the Virtue of Liberality*, Lanham, MD: Rowman and Littlefield, 1996, chapter 1.
8. Martin Buber, 'Distance and Relation' in Maurice Friedman, (trans. and ed.) *The Knowledge of Man: Selected Essays*, New York: Harper and Row, 1965, p. 70. Norton quotes this on p. 11 of *Imagination, Understanding, and the Virtue of Liberality*.

9. Norton, *Imagination, Understanding, and the Virtue of Liberality*, p. 81.

10. Buber, 'Elements of the Interhuman' in *The Knowledge of Man*, p. 85.

11. Buber, 'The Word that is Spoken' in *The Knowledge of Man*, p. 114.

12. See Robert R. Williams, *Recognition: Fichte and Hegel on the Other*, Albany, NY: State University of New York Press, 1992.

13. Amy Gutmann, 'Introduction', *Multiculturalism: Examining the Politics of Recognition*, Princeton, NJ: Princeton University Press, 1994.

14. Gutmann, *Multiculturalism*, p. 24.

15. Charles Taylor, 'The Politics of Recognition' in Gutmann, *Multiculturalism*, p. 73.

16. Derek Parfit, *Reasons and Persons*, Oxford: Clarendon Press, 1984, chapters 6–9.

17. Mohandas K. Gandhi, *An Autobiography: The Story of My Experiments with Truth*, Boston: Beacon Press, 1993, part III: chapters 7 and 8. Augustine, *Confessions*, London: Collier Macmillan, 1961, book VIII.

18. For discussions of sati (also spelled *suttee*) see: Sakuntala Narasimhan, *Sati: Widow Burning in India*, New York: Anchor Books, 1992; Catherine Weinberger-Thomas, *Ashes of Immortality: Widow Burning in India*, Chicago: University of Chicago, 1999; and the essays in John Stratton Hawley, *Sati: The Blessing and the Curse*, Oxford: Oxford University Press, 1994.

19. A recent case of sati occurred in 1987 and was the subject of a legal dispute. Two rival descriptions of this event are described by Susan Abraham in 'The Deorala Judgement Glorifying Sati' (*http://www.hsph. harvard.edu/grhf/SAsia/forums/sati/articles/judgement.html*). One description describes the widow – a 19-year-old girl who had only been married for seven months – as a pious and willing participant. Another describes a coercive male crowd forcing her onto the pyre. Further discussion of this event can be found in essays by Oldenburg and Nandy in Hawley (ed.) *Sati: The Blessing and the Curse*.

20. 'Beyond Tolerance' is the title of Chapter 4 of Norton's book. The idea of exchanging perspectival world views was quoted from Norton, *Imagination, Understanding, and the Virtue of Liberality*, p. 81.

21. Norton admits that human being is 'problematic' in *Imagination, Understanding, and the Virtue of Liberality*, pp. 92–3.

22. Hannah Arendt, *Eichmann in Jerusalem*, New York: Penguin Books, 1977, p. 49.

23. Buber, 'Distance and Relation' in *The Knowledge of Man*, p. 69.

4

Stoic Tolerance

> After all, what is it that frets you? The vices of humanity? Remember that all rational beings are created for one another; that toleration (*anexesthai*) is a part of justice; and that men are not intentional evildoers.
>
> Marcus Aurelius[1]

I turn now to the Stoics in an effort to examine historical models of the virtue of tolerance. Greek terms related to tolerance include words associated with the verbs *phoreo* (to carry) and *anexo* (to hold up). These terms show up in both Marcus and Epictetus and form the basis of the general idea of enduring, bearing or tolerating adversity. I focus here especially on Marcus Aurelius – the Stoic philosopher–king – because he provides a link between the ideals of individual virtue and politic excellence. However, tolerance is not only for philosopher–kings; thus I contrast Marcus with Epictetus, the Stoic philosopher–slave.[2] I conclude that the Stoic virtue of tolerance is useful politically to the extent that it allows individual political agents to pursue justice in a more rational fashion.

The Stoic idea of tolerance is connected with the general idea of mastering the emotions in reaction to external events. This includes reacting properly to the actions of others with whom we disagree. Like us, Roman Stoics were aware of the fact of diversity. Cicero, for example, distinguishes the universal reasonable character of human being from those differences that arise from natural diversity.[3] He recognizes that because individuals are empirically different, the pursuit of virtue will result in diverse human lives. Each person should thus focus on his own duties and character and 'not wish to try how another man's would suit him'.[4] And yet, this diversity is supposed to be held together by the unifying law of reason. The tension between universality and difference is the space of toleration: we tolerate differences, as long as those differences do not violate the principles of justice. The Stoic idea of justice focuses on the universality of natural law: individuals are to be respected insofar as they are members of the natural community of reason within the cosmopolitan world-soul. But this respect does not aim to produce conformity or eliminate diversity.[5]

From this idea of natural law comes an idea of equality before the law that prefigures modern political thought. Although Cicero does claim – through Scipio – that 'nothing is sweeter than freedom, even to wild beasts', it is notoriously difficult to identify in Stoicism the modern liberal notion that the rights of individuals should limit state intervention.[6] The Stoic ideal of a moderate ruler does not develop through a liberal political theory. Rather, it develops from the idea that the action of the ruler should be subordinated to a more pervasive account of ethics and the good life. As Pierre Hadot concludes: 'For Marcus, philosophy does not propose a political program ... In the last analysis, the only true politics is ethics.'[7] This Platonic ideal of philosophy as the ruler's guide of action leads to a sort of tolerance on the part of the ruler. But this is only true insofar as tolerance is a virtue for individuals and especially for the ruler. In this way, moral tolerance provides the ground for political toleration in Stoicism, in a way that is quite different from the more explicitly political accounts of toleration we find in the liberal tradition. This becomes obvious when we note that although Marcus talks about developing the virtue of tolerance, he was actively engaged in persecuting minority sects, including the Christians.

If the Stoic is supposed to cultivate indifference to external matters – including such external indifferents as loss of liberty, loss of property and even loss of life – it is difficult to imagine exactly where the limit of state power might be. Obviously, the idea of toleration that has been developed in modern liberal theory does a much better job of arguing for the limits of state power in light of rights to life, liberty and property. Nonetheless, Stoicism is useful for helping us understand why an individual might strive to be tolerant of others. Indeed, Stoics are ambivalent about politics in general because they realize that a life of quiet contemplation might be the only life that allows for freedom.[8] Perhaps because of the apolitical tendencies of Stoicism, very little attention has been paid to Stoicism in recent discussions of toleration.[9] This is ironic because the fathers of the liberal tradition – Locke, Kant, Jefferson and Mill – were themselves influenced by Stoicism.

In what follows I will not discuss the vexing issue of whether the Stoic sage should take up the task of politics. Rather, I will focus primarily on the question of why any individual – whether slave or emperor – should cultivate tolerance. Along the way, I will distinguish the commitment to tolerance from slavish submission and from relativism. The virtue of tolerance does not result either from impotence or from the abandonment of the idea of universal norms for judgement. Tolerance is possible because we are able to use reason to control our emotions and resist our negative judgements. It is good to be tolerant because tolerance helps fragile, fallible and socially interdependent rational beings develop towards self-sufficiency.

Stoicism: preliminary consideration

The general account of toleration that we find in Stoicism comes from two directions. First, Stoics modestly recognize the limits of our fallible imaginations. Modest assessment of one's own capacity to judge the other can ground toleration towards the other without becoming moral scepticism: modesty does not ask us not to judge the other but merely to admit our limits while refraining from following through on all the negative consequences implied in our negative judgement. In this way modesty and tolerance are part of the philosophical life spent in pursuit of self-knowledge. Second, for the Stoics, the task of philosophy is to help us properly distinguish between those things which are in our power and those things which are not. Tolerance results when we realize that the activities of others are not in our power.

Thus toleration develops from a modest evaluation of our capacity to judge others and from a cultivated indifference towards uncontrollable externalities. This attitude is important for a life of virtue because it helps us to attain self-mastery by allowing us to distance ourselves from pernicious emotions such as anger and resentment, while also cultivating mercy and magnanimity. Tolerance is part of a general search for tranquility and self-control in a world of diversity, conflict, illusion, vanity and ignorance. Thus in Marcus' writings tolerance is part of a much larger idea of 'bearing and forbearing'. This attitude comes from a somewhat bleak appraisal of the human condition, although this melancholic point of view is itself derived from a modest appraisal of our own mortal and fallible lives.

> What is it then, that still keeps you here? The objects of sense are mutable and transient, the organs of sense dim and misled, the poor soul itself a mere vapor exhaled from the blood, and the world's praise, in such conditions, a vain thing. What then? Take heart, and wait for the end, be it extinction or translation. And what think you, is all that is needful until that hour is come? Why, what else but to revere and bless them; to do good to men; to bear with them and forbear (*anexesthai auton kai apexesthai*); and to remember that whatsoever lies outside the bounds of this poor flesh and breath is none of yours, nor in your power.[10]

The way in which Marcus connects tolerance, forbearance and endurance to the search for tranquility points us to a sense of resignation in light of the ubiquity of suffering and the presence of death. We should do our best to help others while admitting that other people are not going to change and may even do us evil.

This ideal may seem to go too far, however. It may seem to lead to a form of self-absorbed egoism in which we withdraw from the public sphere and blithely allow our neighbours to do whatever they want to themselves and to others. This is one of the problems of the ideology of toleration as it is practised in liberal societies: it tends to produce atomized and indifferent individuals who espouse a pernicious form of relativism. It is significant in this regard that Marcus is emperor, a position that does not allow him to withdraw in this way, despite his philosophical interest in resigned equanimity. Tranquility demands tolerance. But Marcus is not a relativist and he is not indifferent to the suffering of others, nor can his position allow him to be. Stoicism maintains that there is a human ideal of virtue that includes human interaction and social responsibility. Indeed a concern for justice demands active intervention in some cases. Nonetheless, the point is that social interaction that is guided by the spirit of tolerance will be both more just and more tranquil.

Caricatures of Stoicism portray the Stoic as completely self-absorbed and indifferent to others. This caricature results, in part, from confusing Stoicism with Epicureanism and Scepticism.[11] Self-control and toleration are important for a Stoic conception of both tranquility and justice. However, while apathy towards those things over which we have no power is a goal, complete indifference to others would hinder our pursuit of the ultimate good for human being, which includes justice, friendship and other social virtues. A Stoic account of toleration must thus link concern for others with an understanding of the need for controlling our own judgements and emotions under a general idea of impartiality.[12] In general, we should be concerned with the good of our fellows because they are 'brothers of reason' engaged in the common human endeavour of leading a good life. However, we should also admit that they will disagree with us and may even offend us. We should not be surprised by this and should learn to ignore such differences when we can so that our anger and disgust do not inhibit our ability to exercise proper self-control, do not cloud our critical acumen and do not undermine the development of a community of philosophical inquiry.

Epictetus

'He is gentle, generous, tolerant (*anektikon*), affectionate.' Give him to me, I accept him, I make this man a citizen, I accept him as a neighbor and a fellow-voyager.[13]

Epictetus and Marcus Aurelius form an interesting pair.[14] One is born a slave; the other is emperor. Despite their different social standing, they both reach similarly modest conclusions about being human. From a deterministic, sociological perspective such modesty is understandable coming from Epictetus, the slave, and is remarkable coming from Marcus, the all-powerful emperor. What unites these two points of view is a commitment to freedom by way of self-mastery. This commitment is what leads them both to tolerance. Epictetus does not directly discuss the issue of tolerance to the same extent as Marcus does, although one can piece together from his writings a tolerant point of view. A question we must keep in mind when looking for tolerance in Epictetus is whether his tolerant attitude is the result of a lack of power to negate those things he views negatively or whether there is some positive reason for him to refrain from negating. As we shall see, in many places Epictetus' approach is something closer to slavish submission to the will of the other than it is to deliberate restraint of the power to negate. When we turn to Marcus, we will see a more genuine form of tolerance insofar as Marcus does manifestly possess the power to negate.

Epictetus' moral point of view can be focused around two claims related to the issue of freedom: the will can be controlled by reason and the external world of appearances is of little consequence. Epictetus repeatedly counsels us to ignore the vicissitudes of external life and to prepare to endure the ills that inevitably afflict us all. Indeed, the practice of philosophy is what prepares us to bear these ills, by teaching us to ignore external appearances.[15] In this sense, Epictetus' approach is, in Isaiah Berlin's words, a 'retreat to the inner citadel' which is antithetical to any robust idea of social life or political freedom.[16] Several passages serve to illustrate Epictetus' point of view. He says, 'Remember that what is insulting is not the person who abuses you or hits you, but the judgement about them that they are insulting. So when someone irritates you be aware that what irritates you is your own belief.'[17] Such an idea is connected to a broadly construed idea of endurance, although it falls short of toleration because it is not clear that such endurance is linked to a deliberate restraint of the urge to negate. It is not clear in Epictetus' case whether the one who tolerates abuse and irritation actually has the power to negate or whether he submits because of some inexorable fate such as illness or lack of social standing. Going further, Epictetus asks us to recognize the point of view of the other: 'When someone acts badly towards you or speaks badly of you, remember that he does or says it in the belief that it is appropriate for him to do so ... Starting from these considerations you will be gentle with the person who abuses you. For you must say on each occasion, "That is how it seemed to him".'[18] Again, it is not clear whether this is slavish submission or whether it is tolerance, although the idea of 'being gentle' seems to imply that the abused party has some capacity for recourse.

Apart from these ambiguous passages, Epictetus does offer us some less ambiguous examples of tolerance. In general, his idea is that we should refrain from judging others: 'Someone takes a bath quickly; do not say that he does it badly but that he does it quickly. Someone drinks a great deal of wine; do not say that he does it

badly but that he does a great deal of it. For until you have dis-
cerned what his judgement was, how do you know whether he
did it badly?'[19] This claim supports something like the argument
for toleration based upon modesty. Here Epictetus asks us to
restrain our tendency to leap to conclusions about the activities of
others out of a sense of modesty about our capacity to judge. Epictetus discusses modesty throughout the *Discourses* under the Greek
term '*aidos*', which in addition to modesty can mean a sense of
shame, self-respect and regard for other. Modesty shows up in conjunction with other virtues such as sociality, fidelity, steadfastness,
intelligence, gentleness and tolerance.[20] The basic idea is that one
must modestly assess one's own situation and abilities in order to
be virtuous.

Epictetus' support of the idea of tolerant restraint towards
others comes from his recognition of the diversity of human
possibilities. He recognizes the fact that the world is made up of
a variety of people each with their own interests and talents:
'Different people are suited for different things.'[21] Although he
is undoubtedly concerned with an idea of a unifying virtue, he
recognizes difference in social position, intelligence and virtue.
In one interesting passage, we find a somewhat submissive or
slavish resignation linked to this relativistic point of view.

> To the rational being only the irrational is unendurable (*aphor-*
> *eton*) but the rational is endurable (*phoreton*) ... Now it so hap-
> pens that the rational and the irrational are different for
> different persons ... For to one man it is reasonable to hold a
> chamber pot for another ... But some other man feels that it is
> not merely unendurable (*aphoreton*) to hold such a pot himself,
> but even to tolerate (*anexesthai*) another's doing so.[22]

From this passage we might conclude that relativism follows from
a lack of courage and strength to remain committed to a concrete
idea of the good. It is as if Epictetus is trying to reconcile himself

and others who are at the low end of the social ladder to the inevitability of oppression. This would not be toleration; it would be resignation.

Viewed in a more positive light, Epictetus recognizes diversity as one of those external facts that must be accepted as we develop towards freedom and self-control. The point is not that diversity is good; it is, rather, that diversity must be accepted if we are to live in this world. Differences must be accepted if we are to avoid being frustrated in our dealings with others. For example, when Epictetus recommends ascetic self-discipline as a virtue, he encourages us to avoid condemning those who are not so disciplined or who are not committed to a life of virtue. With regard to sexual purity, he says: 'But do not be angry or censorious towards those who do not engage in it, and do not always be making an exhibition of the fact that you do not.'[23] Thus the development of freedom requires that we concentrate on those things that are within our power and not get sidetracked by a concern for things over which we have no control. We do not have control over other people, so we must refrain from being annoyed, frustrated and disappointed by their actions. Instead we must learn to develop indifference towards those things we cannot control: 'What upsets people is not things themselves but their judgements about the things.'[24] In order to live well, then, we must learn to judge properly and avoid being pulled around by our immediate emotional response. This is the beginning of tolerance: we must learn to modestly appraise our capacity to judge others and thus restrain our inclination to negate those behaviours and beliefs with which we disagree.

Finally, Epictetus connects this idea of endurance and restraint to philosophical practice as embodied in Socrates. In a section of the *Discourses* entitled, 'Against the Contentious and the Brutal', he praises Socrates' tolerant and patient attitude towards the likes of Thrasymachus, Callicles and even his own wife.[25] Socrates' tolerance is based upon the following: 'Socrates bore very firmly in mind that no one is master over another's governing principle.'[26]

The example of Socrates is an interesting one for it points us to the fact that philosophers, who reason with others and who engage others in dialogue, should nonetheless maintain a tolerant attitude towards their interlocutors. Epictetus thus asks us to reason with one another but he also asks us to modestly assess the power of reason in order to recognize that ultimately we have no power over the opinions of others.

Marcus Aurelius

Epictetus' discussion of tolerance is haunted by the fact that his argument for self-restraint often appears as a rather slavish retreat to the inner citadel. Epictetus does not have the power to negate and so reconciles himself to the world by learning to endure annoyance, abuse and suffering. Such a problem does not occur when we turn to Marcus Aurelius' claims about toleration. Marcus does have the power to negate but he counsels himself to use it with restraint. Like Epictetus, Marcus recognizes certain limits on our capacity to judge others and also recognizes that freedom requires the development of self-control over emotions. He further links tolerance with the goal of critical dialogue. Marcus assumes that human beings are rational and social. We must do our best, then, to help others towards the good of becoming rational. The main way to express our concern for the welfare of our fellows is through philosophical discussion, admonition and persuasion. Indeed, one should not coerce a rational being against his or her will. However, if it is necessary to intervene in the name of justice, we must do so: 'Try to move men by persuasion; yet act against their will if the principles of justice so direct.'[27] Tolerance is, of course, only a part of justice. Occasionally intervention is necessary, although we detect in Marcus the hope – shared by Socrates – that intervention would not be necessary if people were better educated in philosophy and the study of virtue.

Marcus does express reluctance about such intervention. His reluctance to harm others and his desire to help them echoes Seneca's advice to Nero in 'On Clemency': 'Magnanimity becomes every human being, even the lowliest of the low; for what could be grander or sturdier than to beat misfortune back?'[28] Such advice makes sense within the context of Stoicism's understanding of world-citizenship.[29] From the Stoic point of view, even the emperor is merely one part of the whole who shares the capacity for virtue with his 'brothers of reason'. Since the emperor has more power than most, he has an even greater obligation to be magnanimous and tolerant towards those fallible mortals he governs. Seneca concludes: 'For a king, even a raised voice and intemperate language are a degradation of majesty.'[30]

Marcus' claims about tolerance then contain a crucially *political* import. Unfortunately this tolerant philosopher–king was himself involved in the intolerant persecution of Christianity, showing us the need for institutional and procedural limits on state power.[31] In making sense of this, we must recognize that Marcus' philosophical goal – the life of the Stoic sage – was often at odds with the demands of his political life. Moreover, we must recall that the basic idea of monarchy – especially a monarchy headed by a philosopher – was not at odds with the philosophical tradition that extended back to Plato.[32] Of course this does not fully excuse the persecutions sanctioned by Marcus, but makes us aware of the fact that as emperor (or as a Platonic philosopher–king), his duty was to maintain order within the empire. It is not remarkable that in this context certain dissenters and rebels would be persecuted. It is anachronistic to apply our idea of political toleration, with its connection to free speech and dissent, to political practice in the empire. Nonetheless, we might explain Marcus' melancholy as partly resulting from the conflicting demands of these opposed moral and political ideals.

As a moral ideal, tolerance requires both deliberate restraint and rational criticism of those we tolerate. The Stoic follows

Socrates in claiming that evil is a misfortune that results from ignorance.[33] We must use reason to defeat ignorance, partly by avoiding anger and expressions of indignation.

> How barbarous, to deny men the privilege of pursuing what they imagine to be their proper concerns and interests! Yet in a sense, this is just what you are doing when you allow your indignation to rise at their wrongdoing; for after all, they are only following their own apparent concerns and interests. You say they are mistaken? Why then, tell them so and explain it to them, instead of being indignant.[34]

Instead of anger, we owe our 'brothers of reason' an explanation of their wrongdoing so that they may become better. Justice requires philosophical pedagogy, not anger or vengeance.

Marcus' discussion of tolerance is based upon four ways of looking at confrontations with others with whom we disagree.

1 We both may be wrong, in which case I should not condemn the other.
2 I undoubtedly share many ideas in common with my opponent, in which case I should respect our common ideas and our common rational nature.
3 I may have seen the futility of pursuing incessant arguments with those who will inevitably disagree with me, in which case I should be indifferent.
4 It may be the case that the concepts of good and bad simply do not apply in certain instances.

These different perspectives make it easier to be tolerant, to show compassion and generosity to the other. This all comes together in a profound and important paragraph:

> When anyone offends against you, let your first thought be, under what conception of good and ill was this committed?

Once you know that, astonishment and anger will give place to
pity. For either your own ideas of what is good are no more
advanced than his, or at least bear some likeness to them, in
which case it is clearly your duty to pardon him; or else, on the
other hand, you have grown beyond supposing such actions to
be either good or bad, therefore it will be so much the easier to
be tolerant to another's blindness.[35]

Our moral judgements are finite and fallible. Beneath our disagreements, human beings share much in common, especially
reason and a desire for good. Social conflicts are unavoidable.
Within the larger view of things, our petty squabbles do not
really matter. Our views of good and bad are simply our judgements about things; they are not necessarily in the things themselves. In light of all of this, Marcus states: 'All thoughts of blame
are out of place. If you can, correct the offender; if not, correct the
offence; if that too is impossible, what is the point of recrimina-
tions? Nothing is worth doing pointlessly.'[36] Marcus here tries to
straddle the fence between the demands of justice and realism
about social conflict. We should do our best to enact the good but
we should be realistic about our potential for success. Above all we
should respect the other's rational capacity to make moral judgements with which we may disagree: 'Teach them better, if you
can; if not, remember that kindliness has been given you for
moments such as these.'[37]

It is important to note that although Marcus argues that many
of our moral judgements are misguided, he does not defend tolerance by way of radical relativism or scepticism. Rather he maintains that human virtue is the use of reason in pursuit of social life.
We thus have an obligation to criticize our fellows while allowing
them to disagree with us and while recognizing our own limited
capacities for persuasion. He is not a moral sceptic, although he
does modestly recognize human fallibility: 'If a man makes a
slip, admonish him gently and show him his mistake. If you fail to

convince him, blame yourself, or else blame nobody.'[38] Since my virtue is my own, I must not blame the other for his misdeeds. If I become indignant with the other, I must recognize this as a fault in myself and not in the other: 'When you are indignant with anyone for his perfidy or ingratitude, turn your thoughts first and foremost upon yourself. For the error is clearly your own.'[39] Virtue demands that I do my best to help the other; reason demands that I recognize the other's autonomy and my own finitude. Toleration is thus the best response in cases where the limits of justice are not transgressed and tolerance is a virtue, which contributes to both justice and tranquility.

Stoic tolerance

Stoic tolerance is a form of self-control in which we do not allow the foibles of our fellow human beings to distract us from pursuing the common good which includes our obligation to respect our fellows and to work with them in the pursuit of virtue. Stoic tolerance develops from proper control of our negative emotional responses to others. Seneca's *On Anger* is, for example, an attempt to establish the proper relationship between the disruptive emotion of anger and the proper concern and moral outrage that follow from a concern for justice.[40] This Stoic response might seem to foster an inhuman and un-humane apathetic indifference. But more properly understood, Stoicism asks us to develop *eupathia* or *metriopathia*: proper emotion or measured emotion.[41] Complete lack of passion is clearly *not* the conclusion of Stoicism despite caricatures to this effect. As Becker argues: 'no Stoic ever held the view that the sage's life should be empty of affect, emotion, and passion'.[42] Rather, the goal of Stoicism is to restrain passion properly under the guidance of reason. A Stoic conception of proper emotion provides a useful approach to tolerance because it allows us to think of tolerance as a habit of self-control when confronted with difference and disagreement. However, a full conception of toleration requires us to conjoin proper emotion with our duty to criticize others and administer justice.

Stoicism maintains a unitary vision of the good life for human beings. This may seem antithetical to contemporary discourse about toleration, which emphasizes toleration on the part of the value-neutral state as the best way to deal with the fundamental problem of diversity. But Stoicism is not committed to value neutrality. Rather, tolerance is understood as a moral virtue, not as a political idea of impartial procedural justice. Despite the Stoic emphasis on the unity of virtue, however, there is plenty of room within Stoicism for a plurality of goods, as Becker argues.[43] This plurality is possible since there are a variety of goods that can be subsumed under the natural function of being human. Rational autonomy can lead to a plurality of substantive views of the good. Nonetheless, this diversity does not imply that we should be indifferent about the value of these different goods or that we should slip into a form of relativism. Rather, justice requires critical engagement with those we tolerate, even while reason requires proper control of our emotional reactions when confronted by the incorrigible and intransigent. The Stoic position maintains that we should argue with them while admitting that it would be unwise to become indignant and unjust to interfere except where necessary.

Tolerance as a Stoic virtue involves controlling the negative passions in order to engage in fruitful critical moral pedagogy. Stoicism attempts to restrain impassioned revulsion in order to allow us to consider some reason for not negating the other. Restraint of negative judgement makes it possible to see in the other something of value that transcends our feelings of repugnance. Tolerance is thus a habit of social discourse that allows us to engage the rational part of our companions without succumbing to the vicissitudes of our emotional responses so that we can carry out the critical pedagogical task. Indeed, tolerance is based upon moral concern for the well-being of the other as a rational being capable of pursuing virtue in his or her own way. This moral concern is best expressed by overcoming our emotional response to repugnant practices in order to engage the other in philosophical dialogue about the good.

For the Stoic, the best way to contribute to the development of virtue in rational adults is to avoid coercion and, instead, appeal to argument. The primary way in which we avoid manipulation and coercion is by restraining emotional responses in order to focus upon arguments and reasons. Quite simply, emotional responses get in the way of rational criticism. We must also recognize that coercion will not help us to lead others either to moral autonomy or to the truth; we each must reach these for ourselves. Nonetheless, tolerance does not mean mere acquiescence in the face of diversity. Rather, if we think that the development of moral autonomy is good, tolerance requires that we confront those with whom we disagree and exhort, admonish, argue and, in general, attempt to persuade them towards the truth.

It is important to note that Stoic tolerance is part of an individual's own pursuit of virtue. My search for moral autonomy or good requires that I consider other alternative views. I may ultimately disagree with these alternatives; however, I owe it to myself to consider them. As Epictetus counsels: 'It is for this reason that the philosophers advise us to leave even our own countries, because old habits distract us and do not allow a beginning to be made of another custom.'[44] If I want my decisions to be as rational as possible, I should make my decision in the light of as much evidence as possible. Evidence in moral decision-making must include alternative moral choices and the kinds of lives to which these lead.

However, a problem may occur if this imperative is taken alone. It seems to claim that I ought to tolerate immoral behaviour so that I may better understand why it is immoral and thus why I ought not to choose it. Thus my quest for autonomy would come at the expense of some others who are the victims of immoral behaviour (after all, I learn valuable lessons from their mistakes and their pain). To solve this problem we must recognize that the imperative for tolerance cannot be viewed in isolation. It applies only to those opinions about which I may be mistaken. Moreover, it only applies to questions that do not violate the other's search for the good. Indeed, to become an autonomous moral self is to learn to care about the autonomy and good of others. In this sense, we must avoid the 'give them enough rope to hang themselves' problem of indifferent laissez-faire toleration. My moral autonomy depends on the autonomy of others because I rely upon those others to make arguments with me, exhort me, admonish me and, in general, try to persuade me to become autonomous and to pursue the good. My virtue depends upon the virtue of these others because I am a social animal who benefits from virtuous community. To complete my own quest for autonomy and a good life, I should thus encourage the other to become virtuous. If the other is recalcitrant, I should admit defeat and move on, realizing that if they violate justice, I must intervene.

So what should we do about our emotional responses to those with whom we disagree? The question is whether one should be entirely dispassionate or whether we should care about those others who disgust and disturb us. The idea of *eupathia* is useful here. *Eupathia* results as we use reason to see the real causes of disgust and anger. As Epictetus and Marcus both indicate, the cause of an insult or offence is usually not deliberate injustice (which must be punished) on the part of the other but, rather, ignorance in both ourselves and in the other. Emotional responses to those we find repugnant disrupt reason and prevent us from developing understanding. We must control our emotions rationally in order to arrive at a tolerant critical perspective. In some cases, this will help us move beyond an injury: 'Put from you the belief that

"I have been wronged", and with it will go the feeling. Reject your sense of injury, and the injury itself disappears.'[45] In other cases, it will help us pursue justice impartially and mercifully.

The emotions that properly accompany tolerance are thus modesty and compassion. We must restrain ourselves by recognizing the fact that others will disagree with us. If we realize this, then our 'astonishment and anger will give place to pity'.[46] This is not only a form of altruism but is also a matter of self-interest. We need the friendship of other good people to complete our own quest for goodness. Anger and disgust usually serve only to undermine reason, alienate us from others and prevent us from fulfilling our social duties.

Pursuit of the good requires that we rationally criticize our fellows, that we listen to their criticisms of us and that we tolerate their failings when justice does not require active intervention. This involves distancing oneself from one's passions long enough to listen to reason and to examine the arguments made about one's passions. The difficulty for a Stoic social philosophy is thus the same difficulty found in liberal discussions of the paradox of toleration: how do we critically engage each other while not becoming intolerant and while not sacrificing the demands of justice? In Stoicism the answer is found in proper control of the passions such that justice is not obscured by immoderate emotional responses.

Conclusion

Stoicism entered modern political philosophy by way of Spinoza. For Spinoza, virtues of mind such at temperance, sobriety and chastity give us power over our passions.[47] Although Spinoza does not focus on the virtue of tolerance in any detail, it is one of these virtues of mind.[48] It helps us both to attain self-mastery and to properly judge others. Spinoza is significant because he provides a link between a Stoic theory of the emotions and an idea of *political* toleration as developed in his *Theological-Political Treatise*, which may have influenced Locke's account.[49] Both Spinoza and Locke focus on the impossibility of using political power to force people to think in an orthodox fashion. This idea, the root of contemporary liberal ideas about toleration, is thus indirectly linked back to the Stoic idea that reasonable dialogue guided by tolerance is the best way to make our 'brothers of reason' more virtuous.[50]

Justice includes tolerance because we should be merciful and compassionate towards rational beings with whom we disagree. Tolerance is also, however, a virtue of self-sufficiency: I will control myself better if I focus upon those things which I am able to control, i.e., my own opinions and emotions. Stoic tolerance thus results from the fundamental insight that we cannot control the opinions and actions of others. Despite this, we must not become completely indifferent to those others who are essential to the joint project of living a good social life. As Marcus concludes: 'In one way humanity touches me very nearly, inasmuch as I am bound to do good to my fellow-creatures and bear with them. On the other hand, to the extent that individual men hamper my proper activities, humanity becomes a thing as indifferent to me as the sun, the wind, or the creatures of the wild.'[51] Wisdom and tolerance result when we are able to link our obligations to others with this sort of indifference towards those things over which we ultimately have no control.

Notes

1. Marcus Aurelius, *Meditations*, 4.3, trans. Maxwell Staniforth, Baltimore: Penguin, 1969, p. 63. For an alternative translation by A.S.L. Farquharson see Marcus Aurelius, *Meditations* (with an introduction by Andrew Fiala), New York: Barnes and Noble, 2003. For the Greek, I have consulted *The Communings with Himself of Marcus Aurelius Anoninus, Emperor of Rome*, revised text and trans. C.R. Haines, Cambridge, MA:

Harvard University Press, 1961. I have modified Staniforth's translation where appropriate.

2.   For debates about whether Marcus is a 'true' Stoic see Staniforth's introduction to the *Meditations* and R.B. Rutherford, *The Meditations of Marcus Aurelius: A Study*, Oxford: Clarendon Press, 1989. Rutherford argues that Marcus is indeed a Stoic despite the fact that his melancholic, somewhat otherworldly tone sets him apart from earlier Stoics including Epictetus (Rutherford, pp. 219, 227). Also see Pierre Hadot, *The Inner Citadel: The Meditations of Marcus Aurelius*, Cambridge, MA: Harvard University Press, 2001.

3.   Cicero, *De Officiis*, Miller trans., Cambridge, MA: Harvard, 1961, I.xxx–xxxi.

4.   Cicero, *De Officiis*, I.xxx, 113.

5.   As Becker concludes: 'these conflicts appear to be endemic to human social life, and Stoic ethics has no a priori commitment to achieving a complete integration of interpersonal norms, either in theory or practice' (*A New Stoicism*, Princeton, NJ: Princeton University Press, 1998, p. 52).

6.   Cicero, *The Commonwealth*, trans. Sabine and Smith, Indianapolis: Bobbs Merrill Co., 1929, I: 35. See Phillip Mitsis, 'The Stoic Origin of Natural Rights' in Katerina Ierodiakonou (ed.) *Topics in Stoic Philosophy*, Oxford: Oxford University Press, 1999, pp. 153–77.

7.   Pierre Hadot, *The Inner Citadel*, p. 306.

8.   See Cicero, *De Officiis*, I.xx, 69–70.

9.   One exception is Martha Nussbaum's *Cultivating Humanity*, Cambridge, MA: Harvard University Press, 1997.

10.   Marcus Aurelius, *Meditations*, 5.33, p. 89; Haines, p. 126. I have altered the Staniforth translation somewhat in comparison with the Haines translation (Haines, p. 127). This conjunction of *anexesthai* and *apexesthai* is interesting: *apexesthai* means something like holding oneself apart from something while *anexesthai* means holding up as under a burden.

11.   For a discussion of differences among these see Martha Nussbaum, *The Therapy of Desire*, Princeton, NJ: Princeton University Press, 1994.

12.   Julia Annas says: 'The Stoics are the first ethical theorists clearly to commit themselves to the thesis that morality requires impartiality to all others from the moral point of view' (*The Morality of Happiness*, Oxford: Oxford University Press, 1993, p. 265). Annas critiques Stoics as 'unpolitical' (ibid., 311) and notes the mood of alienation found in Marcus and Epictetus (ibid., 175–6).

13. Epictetus, 'Against the Contentious and the Brutal', *Discourses*, 4.5, trans. Oldfather, Cambridge, MA: Harvard University Press, 1959, p. 339. I have altered Oldfather's translation, substituting 'tolerant' for his 'patient'.

14. For a detailed account of the relation between Marcus and Epictetus see Hadot, *The Inner Citadel*, especially chapter 4: 'The Philosopher-Slave and the Emperor-Philosopher'.

15. For example, *Discourses*, 3.10, 'How ought we to bear our illnesses?', p. 71 ff.

16. Isaiah Berlin, 'Two Concepts of Liberty' in *Four Essays on Liberty*, Oxford: Oxford University Press, 1969. Berlin mentions Epictetus in this regard on p. 140. Orlando Paterson makes the same point about Epictetus in *Freedom*, New York: Basic Books, 1991, vol. 1, chapter 15.

17. Epictetus, *The Handbook*, trans. Nicholas White, Indianapolis: Hackett Publishing, 1983, no. 20, p. 16.

18. *Ibid.*, no. 42, pp. 25–6.

19. *Ibid.*, no. 45, p. 26.

20. Epictetus, *Discourses*, 1.28, 2.22, 3.311. See Douglas L. Cairns, *Aidos: The Psychology and Ethics of Honor and Shame in Ancient Greek Literature*, Oxford: Clarendon Press, 1993.

21. Epictetus, *The Handbook*, no. 29, p. 20.

22. Epictetus, *Discourses*, 1.2, pp. 15–17. Orlando Paterson discusses this passage and links it to a slavish idea of forbearance that, Paterson says, is 'a cop-out' (*Freedom*, p. 281).

23. Epictetus, *The Handbook*, no. 33, p. 23.

24. *Ibid.*, no. 5, p. 13.

25. Epictetus, *Discourses*, 4.5.

26. *Ibid.*, 4.5, p. 233.

27. Marcus Aurelius, *Meditations*, 6.50, p. 103.

28. Seneca, 'On Clemency' in *The Stoic Philosophy of Seneca*, ed. and trans. Moses Hadas, New York: Doubleday Anchor, 1958, p. 143.

29. Martha Nussbaum discusses this in *Cultivating Humanity*, chapters 1 and 2 and in 'Kant and Stoic Cosmopolitanism', *The Journal of Political Philosophy* 5:1, 1997, pp. 1–25.

30. Seneca, 'On Clemency', p. 145.

31. Rutherford, *The Meditations of Marcus Aurelius*, p. xvii. John Stuart Mill makes much of this fact in *On Liberty* and uses it as an example of the problem of unrestrained political power (*On Liberty and Other Essays*,

Oxford: Oxford World Classics, 1998, p. 31). While it is difficult to reconcile this fact with Marcus' tolerant philosophical point of view, Marcus' personal tolerance perhaps goes too far in the opposite direction, as seen in the way he deliberately ignored his wife's infidelity and his son's licentious behaviour (Will Durant, *Caesar and Christ*, New York: Simon and Schuster, 1944, p. 430).

32. Cf. Rutherford, *The Meditations of Marcus Aurelius*, especially the section entitled 'The Stoics and the Empire', pp. 59–80.

33. See Nussbaum, *The Therapy of Desire*, p. 335; also see Annas, *The Morality of Happiness*, pp. 178–9.

34. Marcus Aurelius, *Meditations*, 6.27, p. 97.

35. *Ibid.*, 7.26, p. 110.

36. *Ibid.*, 8.17, p. 124.

37. *Ibid.*, 9.11, p. 141.

38. *Ibid.*, 10.4, p. 152.

39. *Ibid.*, 9.42, p. 149.

40. See Nussbaum's discussion in *The Therapy of Desire*, chapter 11.

41. For the problem of Stoic apathy and the difference between *apatheia*, *metriopatheia* and *eupatheia* see F.H. Sandbach, *The Stoics*, New York: Norton, 1975, p. 59–68 or Lawrence C. Becker, *A New Stoicism*, Princeton, NJ: Princeton University Press, 1998, pp. 128–36.

42. Becker, *A New Stoicism*, p. 128.

43. 'In principle, the diversity of possible Stoic lives – and the lives of Stoic sages – is very great' [Lawrence C. Becker, *A New Stoicism* (Princeton: Princeton University Press, 1998), 21].

44. Epictetus, *Discourses*, 3.16.

45. Marcus Aurelius, *Meditations*, 4.7, p. 65.

46. *Ibid.*, 7.26, p. 109.

47. Spinoza, *Ethics*, trans. Andrew Boyle, London: J.M Dent Orion Publishing, 1993, third part, prop. 41, note, p. 122.

48. For a discussion of tolerance in Spinoza see Michael A. Rosenthal, 'Tolerance as a Virtue in Spinoza's Ethics', *Journal of the History of Philosophy*, 39:4, 2001, pp. 535–57.

49. For a discussion see John Christian Laursen, 'Spinoza on Toleration' in Nederman and Laursen (eds) *Difference and Dissent: Theories of Tolerance in Medieval and Early Modern Europe*, Lanham, MD: Rowman and Littlefield, 1996.

50. On the connections and differences between Kant, Spinoza and the Stoics see Martha Nussbaum, 'Kant and Stoic Cosmopolitanism'. For a

different approach, which traces the virtues of liberalism, including tolerance, to Christian sources see James T. Kloppenberg, *The Virtues of Liberalism*, New York: Oxford University Press, 1998, chapter 1.

51. Marcus Aurelius, *Meditations*, 5.20, p. 85.

5

Modern Philosophy and Inward Sincerity: Religion, Existentialism and Pragmatism

Tolerance is often linked to an account of the formation of beliefs that emphasizes that persons must come to believe things for the right reasons and that coercion does little to create genuine belief. This idea has much in common with Socratic pedagogy; but it also has much in common with a post-Reformation understanding of Christianity. In the modern period this approach is linked to the importance of what Locke calls 'inward sincerity': 'Faith only and inward sincerity are the things that procure acceptance with God.'[1] In this chapter I will focus on a range of philosophers who share this approach. The emphasis here will be on the importance of sincerity of conviction. A good reason to tolerate others is because I imagine that they hold their deeply held beliefs with the same sort of sincere conviction that I do. As Marcel concludes: 'I put myself in the other's place such that I can conceive his opinion to be worthy just because of the intense conviction with which he holds it; it may be that my awareness of my own conviction is somehow my guarantee of the worth of his.'[2]

This still leaves open the possibility of the paradox of toleration. It might be the case, for example, that I can acknowledge the other's sincere conviction that I am evil and even imagine the intensity of his belief that he must kill me. Such an acknowledgement would not, of course, lead me to tolerate him. The limits of tolerance are reached when deeply held beliefs lead to violations of the dignity of others. The ability to have sincerely held beliefs is part of what gives human beings their dignity. It is this aspect of human dignity that we respect when we tolerate others.

A further limit to tolerance is discovered in the problem of failures of the moral imagination, as indicated in Chapter 3. The approach I will outline here requires us to imagine the inward quality of the other's beliefs. But there is always risk and uncertainty when we claim to understand the mind of another. We solve this problem by assuming that there are certain universal features of the mind that all humans share. Included here is an ideal of reason, which holds that persons' beliefs should be founded on good reasons. This is a normative claim, made necessary by the recognition that our beliefs are often not well founded. Modern philosophers, following Descartes, focused on clarifying methods of good thinking. Tolerance is required for those who reach different conclusions by the sincere application of the methods of good thinking. This approach does, however, appear to beg certain key questions. One wonders, for example, whether we should tolerate those who think differently than we do. As we shall see, certain assumptions about good thinking are made here including the following: good thinkers have good reasons for their beliefs, they are persuaded by evidence, and they are practically motivated by the conclusions of their reasoning process. The conclusion of this approach is that on-going dialogue and exchange with the other are necessary if I am to come to the conclusion that the other's beliefs are sincerely held in the same way that mine are.

It should be obvious then that the very idea of a dialogue that makes it possible to imagine the sincerity of another's convictions assumes a certain shared standard of reasoning, which would make this dialogue possible. We begin, then, with the assumption that individuals do in fact have sincere convictions that are based upon reasons that can, to a certain extent, be shared. Moreover, to force an individual to renounce such a sincerely held belief would be perceived by that individual as a grievous assault on his dignity. As Spinoza puts this in conjunction with an argument for political toleration: 'Since, therefore, no one can abdicate his freedom of judgement and feeling; since every man is by indefeasible natural right the master of his own thoughts, it follows that men thinking in diverse and contradictory fashions, cannot, without disastrous results, be compelled to speak only according to the dictates of the supreme power.'[3] Our right to be master of our own thoughts is the crucial assumption here: we are each, ultimately, the judge of our own beliefs and we must each be convinced for ourselves according to reasons. We may have good reasons for our beliefs; but if others who are equally reasonable do not share these reasons, then toleration and dialogue are in order.

Descartes, Spinoza and Rousseau

The idea of inward sincerity points us back to Descartes' emphasis on subjective certainty. Although Descartes' emphasis on certainty and the importance of disciplined knowledge shares much with the Socratic tradition and with Stoicism, Descartes' emphasis on subjectivity represents the special new emphasis of the modern period. Descartes' Stoicism can be found in his method as described in the *Discourses*, where he emphasizes self-control and respect for the limits of mortality. His third maxim includes the following points:

> We should change our desires rather than changing the world. The only thing in our power is our own thinking. We should accept our human limitations without regret. We should make a virtue out of necessity. The only thing we truly possess and control is our thoughts. And discipline and practice are required to enact these truths.

Descartes links this to an ideal of the good life that has strong affinities with Stoicism and the Socratic model, which links living well to thinking well.[4] Descartes' basic point is that reason must be used to adjudicate whether our first-order responses to the world are right or wrong, good or bad. Moreover, Descartes emphasizes our fallibility. He concludes the *Meditations* with a reminder: 'we must confess that the life of man is apt to commit errors regarding particular things, and we must acknowledge the infirmity of our nature'.[5]

The political and moral implications of the Cartesian approach are developed by philosophers such as Spinoza and Locke. Spinoza argues that it is not only impossible to deprive a man of the liberty of saying what he thinks; but he also argues that it is impractical on the part of the sovereign power. And Spinoza uses the language of natural right to defend this position, saying that 'everyone has an inalienable right over his thoughts'.[6] It should be noted that Spinoza's conclusions are closely linked to a critique of the 'tyrannical' conjunction of political power and religious authority. He claims that it is 'dangerous to refer to Divine right matters merely speculative and subject or liable to dispute'.[7] We must admit that this begs certain questions against religious authority, assuming that religious truths are merely speculative or disputable. Obviously, many religious believers will not accept this characterization of religious belief.

Thus, the modern philosophical approach to toleration is bolstered by a certain modern reformed understanding of Christianity and religious belief. The basic idea here is that there are certain standards of reason that are universal. Although these standards may lead to proofs for the existence of God – as in Descartes – they cannot resolve disputes about revealed religion. The conclusion is that such disputes require toleration. Some religious believers will simply reject this way of characterizing their faith. From the standpoint developed here, such believers can be tolerated, so long as they respect the bounds of toleration and do not try to impose their views on others.

This culminates in the tolerant deism of Rousseau's Savoyard Vicar. In the 'Confession of the Savoyard Vicar' Rousseau argues against those who spread religious belief intolerantly, including those who proselytize in non-Christian lands. The Vicar claims that it is pride and a certain lack of self-consciousness that leads to intolerance. He claims that it is ludicrous to condemn non-believers in foreign lands who have never been exposed to Christianity. And he argues against forcing others to believe those stories of a revealed religion that they have not grown up with. He argues that such intolerance is unacceptable both because we lack adequate knowledge to assess the claims of revealed religion (whether 'our' religion or 'theirs') and because the claims of revealed religion often run contrary to the common sense of natural reason. He concludes that it is pride that leads people to believe that their version of revealed religion is the true one: 'You see, my son, to what absurdity pride and intolerance lead, when each man is so sure of his position and believes he is right to the exclusion of the rest of mankind.'[8] Rather than this sort of intolerance, the Vicar encourages the natural religion of the heart and respect for the sincerity of belief of others, so long as they do not contravene the basic ideals of the natural religion of reason.

What is interesting about this argument is that the Vicar claims that his view is derived from an emphasis on modesty and self-restraint that is found in both Christianity and Socratic philosophy. In an important passage where he praises both Socrates and Jesus he states the following: 'One ought always to be modest and circumspect, my child – to respect in silence what one can neither reject nor understand, and to humble oneself before the great Being alone who knows the truth.'[9] He argues that modesty and tolerance follow both from a sort of Cartesian scepticism and from the requirements of Divine justice. He concludes with an idea of religious pluralism that demands tolerance, so long as the adherents of these diverse religions possess the proper sort of inward sincerity that is the heart of all religions: 'The essential worship is that of the heart. God does not reject its homage, if it is sincere, in whatever form it is offered to Him.'[10]

In *The Social Contract*, Rousseau defends freedom of conscience and religion more explicitly, while also defending the idea of a 'civil profession of faith', which marks the limit of toleration by appealing to certain basic beliefs that must be shared by all members of the community. While the state has no power to compel citizens to believe anything specific with regard to religion, the state can require citizens to publicly acknowledge the civil profession of faith because this expression of allegiance to the ideas of the community is essential for the proper function of the community. The state does have the power, according to Rousseau, to exclude those who do not share the basic values of civility, which include religious tolerance. Rousseau concludes that the civil profession of faith contains a few positive dogmas (including belief in the existence of God and the eventual punishment of the wicked). But its one negative idea is a condemnation of theological intolerance. With this idea, Rousseau effectively distinguishes Church and state and claims that we should tolerate those religions that also tolerate the religion of others.[11]

One can be, then, both religious and tolerant, especially when religion is conceived of as a religion either of reason, as in Descartes' approach to God, or as a religion of the heart that emphasizes inward sincerity, as Rousseau does. The difficulty of this idea is that it will appear intolerant to religions that are not themselves so tolerantly focused on the religion of reason or the religion of the heart. Thus we must admit that the modern approach assumes a certain ideal of human reason and its limits, one that emphasizes the importance of subjective certainty and that is opposed to intolerant, dogmatically grounded religious belief.

Self-knowledge and the mystery of the person

Modern philosophy's quest for self-knowledge reached its limits in the vexing attempt to define the human person.[12] Post-Cartesian philosophers struggled with the question of whether the self is really as self-grounded and self-transparent as Descartes makes it out to be. Persons are, in general, self-conscious, they use language and they participate in culture.[13] We might also claim, with Martha Nussbaum, that persons have unique access to their own experience.[14] But there are diverse ways in which personhood is developed and expressed.

The fact of diversity leads us to question whether there is any essential content to the idea of the person. Many have in fact concluded that persons are essentially mysterious. One can find this sense of the mystery of the person made explicit in many works of existentialism, psychoanalysis and postmodernism. It is the theme, for example, of Kierkegaard's profound analysis of self-hood in *The Sickness Unto Death*.[15] For Kierkegaard, the self is always in mis-relation to itself, which is why we are in despair. The word Kierkegaard uses to describe this is 'sin'. From this perspective, we are all 'sinners', insofar as we mis-relate both to ourselves and to God. A tolerant Christian conclusion may be drawn from this fact: sinners have no right to condemn one another (as Jesus implies when he demands, 'let he who is without sin cast the first stone').[16] From Kierkegaard and other post-Cartesians, we reach the general conclusion that a self that is a mystery to itself has no right to condemn other selves. The best we can do, from Kierkegaard's perspective, is focus on our own subjective commitment to what we take to be the truth, while admitting the inability to judge the other's subjective commitment.

Kierkegaard's ideas about 'truth as subjectivity' are linked to the idea that to be a person is to be able to commit oneself loyally – with inward sincerity – to a cause. This ability is linked to the ability to reason and the idea of freedom. But to say that persons are free is to leave the content of personhood open. Persons are free to commit themselves loyalty to a wide range of objects of devotion. The plural possibilities of loyalty indicate the need for toleration. In Rousseau's terms, the religion of the heart can manifest itself in various ways, each of which will be tolerable, so long as they are characterized by a certain sort of piety and commitment. The capacity of persons to freely choose their particular loyalties is complicated by the fact of culture. Cultures are products of the free activity of persons and yet they restrict the freedom of persons in significant ways. Freedom to choose one's own self-concept is thus always freedom within limits.

Nonetheless, freedom is a mysterious capacity. It indicates what Sartre might call 'nothingness', exposed only negatively by way of the anguish of self-questioning. But the very idea that a self could ask a question about itself indicates a certain ontological fissure or opacity in the self that every person must experience. This is one of the roots of what Marcel calls the mystery of self. From Marcel's perspective the mystery of the self points us beyond the self to relations with others and eventually towards the ontological mystery itself. While the emphasis on freedom here appears to have much in common with liberal ideas about persons, the ideas of nothingness and mystery point to a deeper level of analysis than mere political freedom. When I encounter my own self-opacity, I encounter the sense of mystery. The sense of mystery is a non-thematic mood that results from certain discursive procedures in which the self takes itself as an object of inquiry: the sense of mystery is the mood of a self who questions itself. The sense of mystery can lead us to be tolerant of others who are also struggling with the mystery of self: we are each doing the best we can to come to terms with our own freedom.

Emerson and James

The idea of tolerance that I am discussing here is linked to ideas about authenticity that are found in a variety of thinkers in the nineteenth and twentieth centuries in America and in Europe. Beginning with Emerson, American philosophers have emphasized the importance of sincerity of belief. Emerson's notion of self-reliance is quite similar to Kierkegaard's ideas about the importance of subjectivity. These ideas develop from an examination of the question of what it is like to believe something sincerely, and especially what it is like to have religious faith. From this perspective, faith is more than mere external conformity; rather, it is existential commitment in which one's whole being is involved. This claim might be extended to discussions of all our beliefs. However, religious faith is the paradigm here because religious faith is about a person's essential self-conception. This is true, for the most part, whether one is a theist or an atheist. The existential and pragmatic approaches to religion lead us to tolerance: one tolerates the beliefs of others because one respects the struggle of the person who is engaged in a quest to become himself in faith. A common feature of the human experience is the struggle to believe and act in a world of risk and uncertainty. Recognition of this common predicament can be the source of tolerance: since we are all struggling without ultimate assurances, we should be tolerant of the different approaches of our fellows. And we should help one another, as best we can, to persevere in the struggle for authentic faith.

For Emerson, religious truth can only be discovered 'from within'.[17] Like Rousseau, Emerson focuses on the idea of discovering the God within. And like Kierkegaard, Emerson emphasizes the importance of subjective conviction, what he calls self-reliance. Emerson equates this subjective focus with the sublimity of the Christian message. Moreover, he expands the idea that truth must be intuited for oneself by oneself beyond the realm of religion and applies it to the idea of truth in general: 'It (truth) is an intuition. It cannot be received at second hand. Truly speaking, it is not instruction, but provocation, that I can receive from another soul. What he announces, I must find true in me, or wholly reject; and on his word, or as his second, be he who he may, I can accept nothing.'[18] Emerson fears the complacency of those dogmatists who claim to possess the truth just as he fears the monotone voice of the crowd and the tendency of civilization and

culture to stifle the flourishing diversity of voices that could prolif-
erate if each one of us pursued our own muse. And yet, he also
recognizes that too much self-assurance, too much inspiration,
too much individuality can be ridiculous. Amid all of this, Emerson recognizes that the philosophical task, the task of intellect, is to
seek the unity that holds together these diverse individualities,
while still allowing for diverse expressions of the self.

In a way that is more explicit than Emerson, William James
offers a defence of tolerance that is linked both to fallibism and to
a recognition of the importance of diversity. In his essay, 'On a
Certain Blindness in Human Beings', James reaches a tolerant
conclusion that 'absolutely forbids us to be forward in pronoun-
cing on the meaninglessness of forms of existence other than our
own; and it commands us to tolerate, respect, and indulge those
whom we see harmlessly interested and happy in their own ways,
however unintelligible these may be to us'.[19] James thus forcefully
acknowledges the irreducible diversity of human lives. This is
especially true with regard to religious experience, as is obvious in
his *Varieties of Religious Experience*, which celebrates diversity in religious experience. James writes: 'Each, from his peculiar angle of
observation, takes in a certain sphere of fact and trouble, which
each must deal with in a unique manner.'[20]

Diversity of religious experience is inevitable given the fact of
diversity of human experience in general. Just as James argued
against monism in other fields, he also argues against monism in
religion: 'We live in partial systems.'[21] His conclusion from this is
tolerant: 'Unquestionably, some men have the completer experience and the higher vocation, here just as in the social world;
but for each man to stay in his own experience, whatever it be, and
for others to tolerate him there, is surely the best.'[22] James links
this to the subjective nature of existential commitment. In 'The
Will to Believe', he emphasizes that with regard to certain important 'live' questions, we simply cannot wait for sufficient evidence.
In such situations, we must choose – we must make the leap of

faith. James is not saying that we can simply choose to believe whatever we want to believe. Rather, his point is that when we are in doubt because we do not have enough information, and when we must decide, we must do our best and commit ourselves. This is quite similar to ideas expressed by Kierkegaard: to suspend belief is itself a form of belief. And to choose to believe is a form of risk. The context of risk is ubiquitous to life; so is the necessity of choice. And so we must choose as best we can. However, given the fallible nature of belief – especially religious belief – James counsels us to be tolerant of the choices of others. He concludes with the following:

> We ought, on the contrary, delicately and profoundly to respect one another's mental freedom: then only shall we bring about the intellectual republic; then only shall we have that spirit of inner tolerance without which all our outer tolerance is soulless, and which is empiricism's glory; then only shall we live and let live, in speculative as well as in practical things.[23]

Royce

Such ideas are also found in the thought of James' contemporary, Josiah Royce. Royce's *The Philosophy of Loyalty* can be read as a manual for tolerance. Royce is interesting because he blends Emersonian idealism with James' empirical pragmatism. And he is interesting because he influenced Gabriel Marcel and thereby the French existentialists. Royce, like Emerson and James, emphasizes the importance of personal commitment. Royce's formulation of loyalty to loyalty is a useful example of the way in which tolerance is linked to our recognition of a person's capacity to form sincere beliefs. We should respect others' loyalties while being loyal to the idea that we are each entitled to our own set of loyalties. The limit of tolerance is reached, however, when someone's loyalties lead them to deny the humanity of others, by violating the higher order principle of loyalty to loyalty. Thus, we should tolerate others who have deeply held beliefs up to the point at which their deeply held beliefs lead them to violate the deeply held beliefs of others.

Royce's philosophy of loyalty is based upon the existential claim that to become an individual each of us must decide to become loyal to some cause. Royce links this to Kant's idea of autonomy as the self giving the law to itself.[24] But Royce, like Kierkegaard, focuses on the concrete emergence of existential commitment as we struggle to become a self by working to actualize our purposes and ideals. Royce understands individuality in terms of negation or exclusion: the individual can be defined in terms of what it is not. However, he notes that this is a meaningless definition unless it is tied to a specific set of negations, which define our positive purposes.[25] This occurs by way of what Royce calls a 'selective interest', which defines the uniqueness of the individual. The individual expresses this selective interest by an act of will in which he selects and acts upon those activities and objects that will be unique to him. This is what Royce calls 'determinate selection'.[26] From this point of view the greatest wrong is not to choose: 'we are all in the wrong in case we have no cause whatever to which we are loyal'.[27]

Royce wants to emphasize the fact that individuals should be free to choose the object of loyalty. This idea of freely chosen loyalty is similar to the Lockean idea of sincerity of belief that is essential to the idea of tolerance. And it aims to found a community of reciprocal tolerance. Since I desire that my right to choose be respected, I should respect the right of others to choose their causes. On a superficial reading, choice and criticism seem antithetical to loyalty and community: the more we emphasize moral choice, the weaker our loyalties and relations to others can become.[28] The problem for understanding Royce's philosophy of loyalty is thus a problem of understanding the connection that Royce wants to make between the commitments of loyalty and the freedom of individualism within the context of community. Royce thus struggles with and against individualism. He argues that individualism – of the sort that might be associated with Nietzsche or Whitman – runs aground when it claims that individuals need not be loyal. Such 'expressive individualism' has much in common with the sort of view that Kierkegaard criticized in his description of the Aesthete in *Either/Or*.[29] An individual who has no loyalty is incomprehensible because he will never become part of a larger community. This idea is as much an ontological claim as an ethical one. For Royce, an individual is always already part of some universe. To be an individual is to locate oneself positively, by active loyal commitment, within this universe. Since this is the task of every individual, individuals should respect each other in the common attempt to become themselves.

Royce is not willing to prescribe which causes we ought to devote ourselves to. This laissez-faire approach is characteristic of American liberalism: the good for human beings is to allow them to devote themselves wholeheartedly to their own freely chosen causes. Royce's idea is related to Emerson's idea of the connection between self-reliance and community. Self-reliant individuals who are loyal to the idea of loyalty – who respect the inward sincerity of others – will be able to create strong tolerant communities.

Tolerance follows from recognition of our inability to fully judge the existential commitment of our fellows. With regard to our fallibility in judging an other's existential commitment, Royce says: 'My statement of the moral principle gives to us all an extremely limited right to judge what the causes are to which any one of our neighbors ought to devote himself.'[30] Each one of us who authentically attempts to become loyal and who respects the moral law that demands loyalty to loyalty should be allowed to pursue our own loyalty in our own way: 'I must leave to the individual the decision as to the choice of the cause or causes to which he is loyal.'[31] And further, I must recognize the limited nature of my own capacity to judge by recognizing that my own perspective is coloured by my own choice of projects, my own set of loyalties and, ultimately, by my own ignorance: 'I may not judge a man to be without an object of loyalty merely because I do not understand what the object is with which he busies himself.'[32] I ought then to tolerate different choices as long as those choices do not violate loyalty to loyalty.

Royce's tolerant ideal is not, however, antithetical to the idea that there is an absolute truth and that there are higher order unities that transcend individual choice and perspective. This is the second key aspect of Royce's point of view and it is one that provides a useful complement to recent merely 'political' versions of toleration. Indeed, it is one that Marcel indicates as providing the link between Royce's philosophy of loyalty and Marcel's own ontological approach. Marcel interprets Royce's idea as follows: 'Here we rediscover, though transposed into the ethical realm, Royce's idea of a single plan which admits of an infinite number of subordinate plans and requires that infinite diversity in order to be itself, so that it needs them and does not determine them by virtue of a mere analytic implication.'[33] This is quite different from the idea of toleration found in contemporary political accounts: it grounds tolerance in a theory of being. For Royce, diversity is necessary for the full development of the whole. In other words, for Royce and, as we shall see, for Marcel, tolerance is the opening in which the conspectus of the whole – what Marcel calls the ontological mystery and what might also be called God – makes its appearance.

Royce makes the move to the whole by indicating that specific loyalties point beyond themselves towards the idea of loyalty to loyalty. In the same way, our finite human causes link together in larger, what Royce calls 'superhuman', wholes. Despite his idealist sympathies, however, Royce remains a fallibilist with regard to truth. Truth requires tolerance of a sort: one must be loyal to loyalty in order to find the truth. Thus Royce links the pursuit of truth with his idea of the 'lost cause': 'Truth is itself a cause, and is largely as one must admit, for us mortals, just now, what we called, a lost cause.'[34] This fallibilism is ultimately what ties Royce most closely to James and pragmatism. Royce concludes:

> We need unity of life. In recognizing that need my own pragmatism consists. Now, we never find unity present to our human experience in more than a fragmentary shape. We get hints of higher unity. But only the fragmentary unity is won at any moment of our lives. We therefore form ideas – very fallible ideas – of some unity of experience.[35]

Tolerance – loyalty to loyalty – is required for the pursuit of truth because we learn from others when we allow them to pursue their own good in their own way.

Marcel

Gabriel Marcel's ideas about creative fidelity borrow from Royce's ideas about loyalty. Both Royce and Marcel focus on loyalty or fidelity as a way in which an individual becomes himself through time. Our loyalties, our faith, our intentions and our projects give us continuity through time. The relation between this idea and the idea of tolerance is found in the fact that while each individual must constitute himself through time, we have a very limited capacity to judge the loyalties and fidelities of others. Moreover, for Marcel, as for Royce, the act of tolerating the other opens the door towards a form of transcendence in which the self and the other can be reunited. Marcel connects the idea of tolerance explicitly to the religious question and the problem of an ecumenical approach to religion. Marcel finds a way to integrate tolerance with faith, love, transcendence and grace. Tolerance fits with values such as truth, fidelity and love insofar as tolerance is an expression of fraternity and respect for human freedom. Marcel writes: 'the fraternal man is somehow enriched by everything which enriches his brother, in that communion which exists between his brother and himself'.[36]

This may sound like a naïve form of social optimism; however, one cannot deny that Marcel knew first hand the horrors of twentieth-century social life. Indeed Marcel acknowledges that modern society can produce a sort of conformity that is antithetical to a genuine respect for human dignity or for the truth.[37] But Marcel insists that truth is poorly served by propaganda and the other methods of producing conformity found in mass society. Marcel goes on to explain in a passage that is reminiscent of Buber that the sort of hope that lies beneath fraternity is the hope of 'mutual education'.[38] When we approach others with this sort of tolerance, which is closely related to love, we look beyond the superficial source of our disagreements to the transcendent mystery of the spirit which underlies our disagreement. Marcel further implies that any transformation of the other will not occur by way of my activities. Rather, they will occur by way of grace or the mystery of being. For this to be accomplished we must refrain from impinging on the solitude of the other because there is 'no respect without distance'.[39]

In *Creative Fidelity*, Marcel undertakes what he calls a phenomenological and dialectical analysis of tolerance. Marcel recognizes the paradox of toleration and focuses on its resolution by turning tolerance into a 'negation of a negation'. For Marcel, tolerance is not itself a primary positive value. Rather, tolerance is a reaction to intolerance. Intolerance is linked to the tendency of human beliefs and institutions to become ossified by orthodoxy and conformity. Just as Kierkegaard criticized 'Christendom', Marcel critiques the dogmatism of 'catholicism'. And he ties his open-mindedness to the New Testament values of charity, humility and love. From Marcel's point of view, those who believe they are in possession of some privileged access to divine truth must not intolerantly condemn the ignorance of others. Even with regard to heresy, Marcel advises humility and charity.[40]

There are several reasons for this tolerant self-restraint. First, the object of religious fidelity is God, who is mysterious and with whom we relate on the level of intersubjectivity. Thus we can never be convinced of faith in the way that we can be convinced of facts about mere 'things'. As Marcel puts it we 'believe in' God; rather, than 'believing that' God exists. Second, the subjective nature of faith and the possibility of error make it necessary to refrain from criticizing the other. The Christian virtues of humility, charity and love are thus explicated in relation to this understanding of faith and its object. We ought to be humble because the object of faith is the transcendent mystery; we ought to be charitable because each individual is struggling with the existential project of faith.

Marcel is not afraid of criticism and debate. Indeed, he recognizes that with regard to mystery, dialogue is necessary. The sort of dialogue he has in mind is similar to Buber's idea of the I–Thou relation. Essential to this is the idea of being open to the presence of the other and through this presence being open to the presence of the transcendent Other: 'Creative fidelity consists in maintaining ourselves actively in a permeable state and there is a mysterious interchange between this free act and the gift granted in response to it.'[41] The word to describe this free interchange is love; and Marcel links love to the idea of generosity and the gift. When Marcel says, for example, 'to give is not to seduce', he articulates a form of tolerance.[42] Because faith is subjective, we have no power over the faith of the other. To think so is to reduce faith to something into which we can be seduced. But this is to misunderstand the nature of faith: we must come to believe for the right reasons and in the right way.

Conclusion

The ideas of this chapter are perhaps most easily applied to the question of tolerance between and among religious believers.

Indeed, toleration developed as a political ideal in the modern West in the context of wars between Christians. Atheism would thus seem to pose a limit for this sort of religious tolerance. In his *Letter Concerning Tolerance*, Locke, for example, denied toleration to atheists because atheists were not supposed to be trustworthy. Royce had suggested that the problematic cases were those who had no loyalty at all, which seems to be the situation that concerned Locke in his exclusion of atheists: they are untrustworthy because they are not committed to the idea of a higher power. Rather, as Locke says, atheism 'dissolves all'.[43] In other words, religious believers may suspect that atheists lack that sort of inward sincerity that has been the basis of tolerance for the thinkers discussed in the present chapter. Indeed, Kierkegaard in describing the rebel who turns against God calls this 'inwardness with a jammed lock' and says that in this form of life 'there is really no inwardness, or in any case none worth mentioning'.[44] The worry is that the atheist turns subjectivity into a principle of self-absorption from which there is no escape. The response to this may be intolerance towards those who seem to lack inward sincerity. The difficulty presented here is another version of the paradox of toleration. Is it possible to tolerate someone who denies that which one believes is the ground of all being and whose inward life seems to lack something essential?

My conclusion is that the sort of tolerance that focuses on inward sincerity need not be explicitly tied to any final decision about religious belief. The problem then is not whether one is a theist or an atheist but whether one really does possess inward sincerity. It is interesting to note that while the theist, Marcel, derives his views from Royce's loyalty to loyalty, atheistic humanists such as Paul Kurtz can also appeal to Royce as a foundation for tolerance. Kurtz agrees with Royce that one needs to commit oneself to a cause. Like Royce, he also advocates tolerance. But Kurtz believes that atheists are more tolerant than theists. Kurtz focuses on the problem of fanatics and terrorists who are willing to 'maim and kill innocent humans in order to excoriate wickedness and achieve a better world'.[45] From Kurtz's point of view, this sort of intolerant fanaticism is usually associated with religious belief. However, the point I want to make here is that both theists and atheists can develop tolerance and that both theists and atheists can display fanaticism and intolerance. Rousseau would agree. He argues, in agreement with Pierre Bayle, that 'fanaticism is more pernicious than atheism'.[46] It is not the content of the belief that matters when it comes to theological questions; rather, it is the spirit of inward sincerity with which we pursue belief. At issue, then, is not atheism or theism *per se*. Rather, it is the quality of one's convictions and the virtues that accompany them.

The point here is that one can be sincere in one's beliefs without being intolerant towards others who do not share them. Yes, this does verge towards the paradox of toleration. Of course, there are limits here: when the other – whether he be theist or atheist – is engaged in a campaign to exterminate me, or when he violates the human rights of others, I can no longer tolerate him. However, within a broad range of beliefs and activities, tolerance expresses both my respect for the other and my understanding of the nature of belief, including an understanding of the existential struggles in which we all are engaged.

Marcel's dialogical approach emphasizes that a tolerant dialogue must avoid being a one-sided monologue.[47] One comes to truth through the interchange of divergent opinions. For this to work, one must be 'open' to the other in a way that is not possible for the person who is fanatically convinced of the truth of their opinions: 'When a man says that he is convinced, he puts up a sort of barrier.'[48] What Marcel calls 'faith' – as opposed to conviction – is supposed to be open and not closed in this way. Marcel seems to recognize the problem of the sort of fanaticism that becomes intolerant and even violent when it attempts to engage in 'dialogue': 'The fanatic, in as much as he is a fanatic, ceases to be an interlocutor, and becomes only an adversary who handles what he calls his ideas as offensive weapons.'[49] When I force my views on the other in a fit of zealotry, I betray my God by imposing on the other 'a loathsome image of the God whose interpreter I say I am'.[50] We can avoid fanaticism and develop tolerance by reminding ourselves of the existential importance of inward sincerity, by recalling the mysterious nature of the self, by noting the mutual permeability of those who engage in the dialogue and, finally, by understanding the way in which tolerant communities can develop despite difference.

Notes

1. John Locke, *A Letter Concerning Tolerance*, in Steven M. Cahn (ed.) *Classics of Modern Political Theory*, New York: Oxford University Press, 1997, p. 304.

2. Gabriel Marcel, *Creative Fidelity*, New York: Fordham University Press, 2002, p. 214.

3. Spinoza, *A Theologico-Political Treatise*, New York: Dover, 1951, chapter 20, p. 258.

4. See Descartes, *Discourse on Method*, Part Three in *Discourse on Method and Meditations on First Philosophy*, Indianapolis, IN: Hackett Publishing, 1998, p. 16.

5. Descartes, *Meditations on First Philosophy*, Meditation Six in *Discourse on Method and Meditations on First Philosophy*, p. 103.

6. Spinoza, *Theologico-Political Treatise*, chapter 18, p. 241.

7. *Ibid.*

8. Rousseau, *Emile*, New York: Basic Books, 1979, p. 306.

9. *Ibid.*, p. 308.

10. *Ibid.*

11. Rousseau, *The Social Contract and Discourse on the Origin of Inequality*, New York: Washington Square Press, 1967, pp. 146–7.

12. For a brief discussion see Tom L. Beauchamp, 'The Failure of Theories of Personhood', *Kennedy Institute of Ethics Journal*, 9:4, 1999, pp. 309–44.

13. Charles Taylor links the linguistic, cultural and self-conscious aspects of personhood in his essay 'The Person' in Michael Carrithers *et al.* (eds) *The Category of the Person: Anthropology, Philosophy, History*, Cambridge: Cambridge University Press, 1985.

14. Nussbaum calls this the 'capabilities approach'. See Martha C. Nussbaum, *Women and Human Development*, Cambridge: Cambridge University Press, 2000; and also her discussion in 'Aristotle, Politics, and Human Capabilities', *Ethics*, 111, October 2000, pp. 102–40.

15. Søren Kierkegaard, *The Sickness Unto Death*, ed. and trans. Howard V. Hong and Edna H. Hong, Princeton, NJ: Princeton University Press, 1980.

16. *John*, 8.7.

17. 'It is of no use to preach to me from without. I can do that too easily myself. Jesus speaks always from within, and in a degree that transcends all others' (Emerson, 'The Oversoul' in *The Essential Writings of Ralph Waldo Emerson*, New York: Modern Library Classics, 2000, p. 246).

18. Emerson, 'Harvard Divinity School Address' in *Essential Writings*, pp. 66–7.

19. William James, 'On a Certain Blindness in Human Beings' in *Talks to Teachers on Psychology and to Students on Some of Life's Ideals*, Cambridge, MA: Harvard University Press, 1983, p. 149.

20. William James, *The Varieties of Religious Experience*, New York: The Modern Library, 1994, p. 530.

21. *Ibid.*, p. 531.

22. *Ibid.*

23. James, 'The Will to Believe' in Walter Kaufmann (ed.) *Religion from Tolstoy to Camus*, New York: Harper Torchbooks, 1964, p. 238.

24. Royce, *Philosophy of Loyalty*, Nashville, TN: Vanderbilt University Press, 1995, p. 14.

25. Royce, *The World and the Individual*, New York: Dover Publications, 1959, p. 452 ff.

26. *Ibid.*, p. 460.

27. Royce, *Philosophy of Loyalty*, p. 94.

28. See R.T. Allen's critique of Royce 'When Loyalty No Harm Meant', *Review of Metaphysics* 43:2, 1989, pp. 281–94.

29. The term 'expressive individualism' is borrowed from Robert Bellah *et al.*, *Habits of the Heart*, Berkeley, CA: University of California Press, 1989. Also see Charles Taylor, *Sources of the Self*, Cambridge, MA: Harvard University Press, 1989, chapter 21.

30. Royce, *Philosophy of Loyalty*, p. 94.

31. *Ibid.*, p. 95.

32. *Ibid.*, p. 96.

33. Gabriel Marcel, *Royce's Metaphysics*, Chicago: Henry Regnery Co., 1956, p. 116. Marcel also says that Royce is 'to be credited with realizing very clearly the supra-personal character of the cause to which the loyal soul dedicates himself' (*The Existential Background of Human Dignity*, Cambridge, MA: Harvard University Press, 1963, p. 68).

34. Royce, *Philosophy of Loyalty*, p. 158.

35. *Ibid.*, p. 159.

36. Marcel, *The Existential Background of Human Dignity*, Cambridge, MA: Harvard University Press, 1963, p. 147.

37. See Gabriel Marcel, *Man Against Mass Society*, Chicago: Henry Regnery Co., 1967.

38. Marcel, *The Existential Background of Human Dignity*, p. 148.

39. *Ibid.*, p. 158.

40. Marcel, *Creative Fidelity*, p. 193.

41. Marcel, 'On the Ontological Mystery' in *The Philosophy of Existentialism*, New York: Citadel Press, p. 38.

42. Gabriel Marcel, *Mystery of Being: Faith and Reality*, vol. 2 of the Gifford Lectures, Lanham, MD: University Press of America, 1979, p. 118.

43. Locke, *A Letter Concerning Tolerance*, p. 313.

44. Kierkegaard, *The Sickness Unto Death*, pp. 72–3.

45. Paul Kurtz, *Embracing the Power of Humanism*, Lanham, MD: Rowman and Littlefield, 2000, p. 126. An explicit reference to Royce's philosophy of loyalty is on the previous page.

46. Rousseau, *Emile*, p. 317, footnote.

47. Marcel, *Creative Fidelity*, p. 217.

48. Marcel, *The Mystery of Being*, 2:76.

49. *Ibid.*, 2:115.

50. Marcel, *Creative Fidelity*, p. 219.

6

Existentialism and Repressive Toleration

When, after Marx, the rumor began to spread and gain strength that freedom was a bourgeois hoax, a single word was misplaced in that definition, and we are still paying for that mistake through the convulsions of our time. For it should have been said that bourgeois freedom was a hoax – and not all freedom. It should have been said that bourgeois freedom was not freedom or, in the best of cases, was not yet freedom.

Camus[1]

The theory and practice of liberal toleration can conceal a form of repression that stifles genuine dissent in the name of a supposedly 'tolerant' consensus. This idea was the focus of the Marxist critique of the ideology of bourgeois freedom. And it has been taken up in the ideas of Critical Theorists in the twentieth century. This critique reminds us of the need for reasons for tolerance that are existentially grounded. We saw such approaches in the Stoic emphasis on virtue and in the modern philosophical and religious emphasis on inward sincerity. In this chapter we will consider the views of atheistic French existentialists. These thinkers link the question of private individual freedom dialectically to the fact of political and cultural domination. And they remind us that respect for human transcendence can be joined with the task of developing human solidarity. However, as we shall see, tragedy haunts such solidarity, as communities of critical tolerance may devolve into communities of indifference and barely tolerant silence.

The French existentialists I will discuss here develop toleration from self-consciousness about transcendence, from a commitment to freedom, from recognition of the alterity of the other and from critical resistance to dogmatism and totalitarianism. Moreover, these authors followed Marx in their awareness of the fact that the ideology of liberalism is always at risk of falling into bad faith when it views freedom as a value in isolation from the totality of other values. As Camus says, it is not freedom that is the problem, but bourgeois freedom, and its tendency to understand toleration as openness only to the choices presented by the theory and practice of liberal-capitalism.

I should note at the outset that I am not attempting to present a synthetic account of French existentialism, nor am I attempting to resolve the dispute between Sartre, Merleau-Ponty and Camus over the justification of political violence.[2] Rather, I want to apply the basic insights of this strand of existentialism to the problem of toleration. Of course there is no such thing as existentialism *per se*: differences between the atheists discussed in this chapter and the theistic existentialists discussed in the previous chapter make this clear. Although there are many reasons that toleration is good, the approach discussed here focuses primarily on the experience of transcendence and finitude in light of the problem of ideology and self-deception.

This approach is different from the standard liberal approach to tolerance. John Stuart Mill, for example, emphasizes that individuals know their own interests best and are motivated to actualize these interests for themselves. Thus individuals are supposed to be as free as possible within the limits established by the harm principle. The liberal approach has been criticized by critical theorists as ideological because liberal toleration and its subjectively defined idea of harm cannot account for ideologically driven disputes about harm. Because of the power of ideology, oppressed subjects may not in fact experience themselves as oppressed and so may not realize that they are not being tolerated. This idea goes back to Marx and his claim that the bourgeois notion of freedom conceals various forms of oppression. In the twentieth century, Herbert Marcuse claimed that liberal toleration conceals various forms of intolerance. Marcuse argued that real toleration and genuine respect for autonomy require real equality and objective freedom. Diverse voices must be able to be heard *in fact*, not merely *in theory*. Marcuse argued that American society of the 1960s was not yet tolerant. To support this claim he cited the power of business and the consumer society; the power of manipulative media and advertising; the hegemony of the military-industrial complex; the lack of voices truly critical of the status quo; and a lack of a true commitment to moral education. Marcuse claims that ultimately a tolerant society must *actively support* 'the small and powerless minorities which struggle against the false consciousness'.[3] He concludes that, in the 'society of total administration', the only way for the state to foster the further development of moral autonomy is for it to withdraw tolerance of 'regressive movements' and for it to practise 'discriminatory tolerance in favor of progressive tendencies'. He recognizes that this 'would be tantamount to the "official" promotion of subversion'.[4] Nonetheless, he argues that this is the way a truly liberal state must practise tolerance: by supporting diversity so that citizens are actually allowed to develop self-critical moral autonomy, even to the extent that citizens become critical of the repressive hegemony of the status quo. Recently Slavoj Žižek has expressed a similar idea in his claim that tolerant liberalism deprives radical critique of its political sting: 'Systematic politics is always ready to listen to their [the radicals] demands, thus depriving them of their proper political sting. The system is by definition ecumenic, open, tolerant, ready to listen to all; even if one insists on demands, they are deprived of their universal political sting by the very form of negotiation.'[5] Adorno puts this same critical point in another way: 'The bourgeois, however, is tolerant. His love of people as they are stems from his hatred of what they might be.'[6] In other words, we tolerate 'the other' in order to prevent him from becoming truly other.

One wonders, then, if it is possible for toleration not to be a disguise for repressive power. As noted in the previous chapter, toleration in the modern tradition assumed a certain view of what is reasonable. This ideal conceives of certain sorts of religious belief as speculative and disputable. States that enforce this idea and seek to prevent such 'speculative' religious belief from entering into public discourse – i.e., modern secular states – may in fact appear as repressive to religious believers. Toleration might be, as Adorno hints, an insidious attempt to assimilate the other in order to prevent the other from becoming fully autonomous.

A related worry, from the standpoint of existentialism, is whether toleration is a type of bad faith, self-deception or cowardice. We discussed a similar problem with regard to Epictetus: is toleration a sort of slave-morality or is it a positive good that promotes genuine human flourishing?

Existential writers are especially interesting because they provide us with good reasons to be tolerant, while also recognizing these sorts of problems. One might begin to think about toleration in the context of existentialism by noting the history of toleration as developed within an existential approach to religious faith that focuses on the subjectivity of faith, as noted in the last chapter. However, religious tolerance in the Christian tradition tends to be subordinated to the higher, more positive, values of love, charity and humility. This approach is paradoxical insofar as we are told to love our enemies and to love those who sin. This approach ultimately asks us to overcome negative reactions to the other and replace these reactions with positive affirmation. And so it tends to set up an impossible ideal that can leave us guilty, anxious and in need of grace.[7] A non-religious approach to tolerance need not go so far in the direction of paradoxical love of enemies, although, as we shall see, even the atheistic existentialists advocated a form of tolerance that flirted with more positive values such as love.

Existentialism is a useful resource for understanding toleration because it stresses autonomy and finitude, respect for the alter ego, fallibilism and the modesty that comes from the attempt to assert oneself against one's immediate emotional responses as well as against the prevailing social norms. At their best, existentialists are aware of the tendency of human beings to totalize and terrorize the other. Merleau-Ponty admits as much towards the end of his discussion of terrorism:

> Doubt and disagreement are facts, but so is the strange pretension we all have of thinking the truth, our capacity for taking the other's position to judge ourselves, our need to have our opinions recognized by him and to justify our choices before him – in short the experience of the other person as an *alter ego* in the very course of discussion.[8]

As an antidote to the problem of totalization and terrorism, existentialism's ultimate ethical goal is, as David Cooper has argued, an ethic of 'reciprocal freedom'.[9] The idea of reciprocal freedom is basic to the idea of toleration, even though tolerance is a virtue of the self that need not be reciprocated.

Existentialism begins from an examination of the ego and its experience of itself and the world around it. This examination emphasizes what Sartre calls transcendence, nothingness and freedom. In fact, Sartre's analysis of the negating activity of consciousness fits quite well with the negative structure of toleration. Sartre's discussion of anguish emphasizes the fact that 'man is always separated by a nothingness from his essence'.[10] At issue here is the possible negation of one's immediacy or previous self-concept. This is called anguish precisely because such a negation poses risks to the self and whatever justification it had for its concept of itself: 'My freedom is the unique foundation of values and nothing, absolutely, nothing, justifies me in adopting this or that particular value . . . As a being for whom values exist, I am unjustifiable.'[11] Toleration, as a possibility of self-expression, i.e., as the negation of one's initial negative judgements towards an other, is thus always an anguished risk. We disapprove of the activities of the other and yet, in the space made possible by self-conscious transcendence, we must decide whether to resist turning this initial negative reaction into action. The tolerant sublation of the initial negative response thus indicates that the tolerant self has moved beyond immediacy to the level of self-consciousness. The possibility of toleration is thus an important indication of the fact that self-consciousness is a type of transcendence that includes both freedom and anguish.

A preliminary normative conclusion might be that we should tolerate one another because we are transcendent to ourselves. But the difficulty here is exactly why the possibility of transcendence leads to toleration. Before turning to this question in earnest, let us note that there are some who deny the sort of transcendence described here. Existentialism is opposed to those sorts of dogmatism that postulate a permanent essential self. This is the basic idea that existence precedes essence. At its extreme, existentialism is a form of permanent revolution, what Camus has characterized in *The Rebel* as rebellion against dogmatic claims about the essential self that come from social or religious authorities. This rebellion culminates in radical responsibility that opens onto toleration: 'We have to live and let live in order to create what we are.'[12] For Camus, this tolerant recognition of the other occurs when we resist the emotional temptation that inclines us to remain with final dogmatic claims about the other or about the self. Such claims are the basis of intolerance. Resistance to intolerance is made possible by transcendence. The best we can do, argues Camus, in his work *Neither Victims nor Executioners*, is to wake up and lucidly question the murderous tendencies of intolerant ideologies that offer final solutions to the problem of being human: 'The problem is not how to carry men away; it is essential, on the contrary, that they not be carried away but rather that they be made to understand clearly what they are doing.'[13] We must resist the initial negative judgements to which we are all susceptible and the immediate inclination to destroy the thing we despise. For Camus, we do this by way of self-consciousness about our own tendencies towards fanaticism.

The difficulty here is that existentialism flirts with relativism. Lucidity leaves us with the absurd universe of Camus' Sisyphus.[14] By beginning from the ego and by rejecting universal dogmatism, the existentialist must postulate toleration in terms of personal freedom and responsibility; but he cannot appeal to toleration as an absolute value. The danger is that if freedom and responsibility are personal, then it makes prescriptive claims about toleration hard to come by. Indeed, toleration cannot become a permanent political idea without slipping towards a form of repressive toleration. The difficulty for existentialism is to bridge the gap between the 'I' and the 'we', between transcendence and political ideology. Unlike Stoicism, which postulated an essence for human being that included a set of virtues among which we might find tolerance, existentialism refuses to play the game of postulating a human essence. Nonetheless, tolerance emerges in existentialism from the recognition that the 'essence' of the self is to be engaged in the process of creating an 'essence' in concert with others who are engaged in the same process.

The danger of repressive toleration is the tendency to identify an essence in the name of tolerance, which then becomes intolerant. When governments and institutions defend their ossified structures in the name of toleration, existential toleration has already been sublated. Existential toleration is the openness of individuals who directly encounter one another in pursuit of freedom; it is not the institutionalized formal freedom of governments and laws. Governments and institutions do not transcend themselves in the way that individuals do. Thus, institutionalized toleration tends to become repressive as it incorporates all difference within the limited range of the given possibilities for liberty, even in the name of toleration.

One of the conclusions of existentialism is that we are all, in part, strangers to ourselves. We can and do identify ourselves in cultural terms: as white, black, straight, gay, Christian, Jew or atheist. But these designations can become intolerant when they serve to deny freedom. Each individual is more than the union of these designations. Human persons are free beings with a capacity to choose among the given array of cultural designations. Of course, we are not radically self-choosing: our choosing is finite and contingent. Nonetheless, the possibility of choice is implied by the negative power of transcendence, as is the possibility of tolerance. Just as I can choose to be Christian or not, I can also choose to tolerate Christians or not. It is certainly true that Western liberalism occasionally over-emphasizes the fact that the self is a project of its own freedom; and there are good criticisms to be mounted against a radically isolated atomic form of individualism. But, it seems hard to deny that selves are, in some limited sense, self-choosing. Such an assumption is crucial to the very idea of toleration: the idea of toleration assumes that we can choose not to actualize our initial emotional repugnance towards the other whom we come to tolerate. In this sense, the existential approach is quite close to the liberal approach of someone like Mill. The chief difference, however, is that while Mill assumes that the self knows what is in its own best interest, the existential approach admits that the self-consciousness can be obscured by self-deception and ideology.

The problem of liberalism then is not that liberalism emphasizes autonomy. But rather, that it thinks that autonomy is obvious and easy to obtain. Autonomy, from the standpoint of an easy-going liberalism, thus comes to mean choosing among the limited range of possibilities presented by the liberal-capitalist system. Zygmunt Bauman puts this as follows: 'In the land of individual freedom of choice, the option to escape individualization and to refuse participation in the individualizing game is emphatically not on the agenda.'[15] Tolerant societies do not tolerate those who question whether they are actually as tolerant as they claim. We will tolerate you if you are with us; but if you are against us, we will not. This dichotomizing approach is resisted by the existential emphasis on the very difficulty of becoming a self. Easy dichotomizing leads us to ignore the difficulties each of us discovers as we make judgements in the midst of uncertainty and risk.

Liberal political thinkers recognize the problem of toleration in the so-called paradox of toleration. One form of this paradox asks whether the tolerant should tolerate the intolerant. The obvious answer is no. But the problem is whether it is ever entirely obvious who is tolerant or who is not. Toleration is not a neutral idea. The tolerant need not tolerate the intolerant. However, we are far from clear about who has the moral high ground when toleration itself becomes a political fetish, i.e., when those who hold political power use that power to define who is and who is not tolerant. The existential question is a question that arises prior to or outside of the political question. Existential toleration calls into question the very idea that toleration is something that can be institutionalized in such a way as to make it easy. Indeed, existential toleration is lost when it is appropriated by an institutionalized 'essence'.

Transcendence and truth

For Sartre and other existentialists, the very idea that I could ask a question about who I am implies a certain ontological fissure or opacity in the self in the experience of transcendence that results when a self questions itself. The problem for theists such as Kierkegaard is that for the self to become itself it must relate itself to the relation that sustains, it must 'rest transparently in the power that established it'.[16] This solution of faith is the relation to God. From Nietzsche's quite different atheistic perspective, however, the self is a creation or interpretation of experience that is loaded with history and is the result of a certain moral impetus. The idea of a moral self is an idea that has been bred into us by a moral culture that wants us to believe that there is a substance that is ultimately responsible for its actions. Nietzsche concludes that ' "the subject" is the fiction that many similar states in us are the effect of one substratum'.[17] Heidegger took up the problem of the self when he discussed, for example, 'the nothing' into which Dasein is projected.[18] For Heidegger, the self is a transcendent beyond of being, an *ek-stasis* of being. As such the self is not knowable as a being but is understood in terms of its existence. Although we can try to grasp our existence and authentically be ourselves, this project is always accompanied by the 'dread' which discloses the nothingness of our own existence. In other words, to be a self is to be engaged in a struggle to recognize the nothing that is the self. From Marcel's perspective, as discussed in Chapter 5, the mystery of the self points us beyond the self to relations with others and eventually towards the ontological mystery itself. For Sartre, as already mentioned, consciousness is nothingness. More specifically, 'the permanent possibility of non-being, outside us and within, conditions our questions about being'.[19]

If such descriptions of the self are plausible, they give us a reason to develop toleration towards one another. If one can identify one's own sense of transcendence with the transcendence of the other, then we have the potential for developing a tolerant community, even though this community is one in which we acknowledge our differences.

In Camus' approach to this problem, the self is postulated as a self-creating being. The demands of autonomous self-creation lead to rebellion against external authorities. However, since human rebellion occurs in a social context, the rebel postulates the value of rebellion as a universal value: 'when he rebels, a man identifies himself with other men and so surpasses himself and from this point of view, human solidarity is metaphysical'.[20] In a common struggle against a common enemy, we discover our freedom together and our solidarity: 'I rebel – therefore we exist.'[21]

However, since it is precisely freedom that is discovered to be our shared value, rebellion leads to tolerance: 'To the "I rebel, therefore we exist" and "we are alone" of metaphysical rebellion [i.e., atheism], rebellion at grips with history adds that instead of killing and dying to produce the being that we are not, we have to live and let live in order to create what we are.'[22] Individuals who are each pursuing freedom should leave each other alone, provided that each tolerantly allows the other to pursue his own freedom.

Camus' conclusion sounds quite like Mill's. However, while Mill is sanguine about the salutary effect of liberty on opportunities for human flourishing, Camus, like Kierkegaard and Sartre, recognizes that freedom is a project of fear and trembling. Despite this difference, existentialism is closely linked to liberalism in that it is opposed to those pursuits of freedom that have resulted in what Isaiah Berlin has called 'positive liberty'. The existential critique of totalitarianism comes from a denial of the idea of a human essence. Totalitarian claims about positive liberty are linked to claims about authority and essence that, for existentialists, are never justified. As Beauvoir states, 'the genuine man will not recognize any foreign absolutes'.[23]

It is up to us to become free and to know the truth. We cannot rely on external authorities. Sartre goes so far as to indict God, Stalin and Hitler in one paragraph where he claims that such authorities prevent us from being responsible for the truth. Totalitarian regimes and dogmatic religions give us the truth as a matter of grace: 'Consequently, we are no longer responsible for the true.'[24] But for Sartre, the existential problem is that we are always responsible for the truth insofar as we affirm our freedom. Thus the way to be responsible before the truth, the way to affirm the human condition, is to modestly admit ignorance and tolerantly strive for solidarity: 'All truth is presently provided with an outside that I will forever not know ... I can proudly affirm that I am the one through whom this truth surges up in the world, in modesty I must freely recognize that this truth possesses an infinity of facets that escape me ... Therefore the attitude of generosity throws the truth to others so that it becomes infinite insofar as it escapes me.'[25] Despite this fallible, modest and generous approach, Sartre is not a relativist. The world of facts exists; I do not create the world of facts. Nonetheless, the problem is one of communication. With regard to any truth, 'I do not know what the other is doing with it.'[26] Thus I must admit my own ignorance and turn to the other with what Sartre calls generosity, which is closely related to tolerance.

Quite often toleration is understood as a condescending attitude: I am right but I will permit you to continue with your mistaken practices and point of view. This element of condescension evaporates in light of the mystery of transcendence. As Sartre recognizes in his discussion of bad faith – we are all struggling to be ourselves despite the fact that, as finite temporal beings, we do not fully know ourselves. We cannot blame another or praise ourselves with any justification because we are always in the midst of the struggle: 'How then can we blame another for not being sincere or rejoice in our own sincerity, since this sincerity appears to us at the same time to be impossible?'[27] My sense of transcendence leads me to tolerate you because I am not sure of myself. If I also recognize that you are struggling with your own transcendence then I can even develop compassion for you. Camus discusses this at the end of *The Rebel* in a remarkable passage that links rebellion with generosity and love. He writes:

> Then we understand that rebellion cannot exist without a strange form of love. Those who find no rest in God or in history are condemned to live for those who, like themselves, cannot live: in fact, for the humiliated ... This insane generosity is the generosity of rebellion, which unhesitatingly gives the strength of its love and without a moment's delay refuses injustice.[28]

Sartre makes much the same point in his essay 'The Humanism of Existentialism' by linking the pursuit of personal freedom with a universal respect for the freedom of others: 'Freedom as the definition of man does not depend on others, but as soon as there is involvement, I am obliged to want others to have freedom at the same time that I want my own freedom.'[29]

Critics of existentialism attack it for being egoistic or even solipsistic, as well as for being a sort of relativism. However, with regard to the accusation of egoism, it is important to note that the recurrent theme of existentialism is human solidarity. Existentialists recognize that freedom does not occur in solitude: 'Man can find a justification of his own existence only in the existence of other men.'[30] The primary value of a community of free beings is toleration: to allow the other to be free. And existentialists are not relativists. They link toleration to self-criticism and dialogue in pursuit of truth and authenticity. Nonetheless, they are fallibilists and use fallibilism to resist dogmatism. Beauvoir claims, for example, 'morality resides in the painfulness of indefinite questioning'. She concludes: 'What distinguishes the tyrant from the man of good will is that the first rests in the certainty of his aims, whereas the second keeps asking himself, "am I really working for the liberation of men?"'[31] The recognition of fallibilism points beyond relativism towards the primary philosophical value, which is to love the truth: 'To love the true is to enjoy being ... To want the truth is to prefer being to anything else, even in a catastrophic form, simply because it is.'[32]

The truth of existence is found in concrete projects, goals and activities in the world. There is an interplay here between facts and interpretations. The world is as it is; and yet, reality is in part constituted by our projects. The world opens itself to us, the truth is exposed, only in light of the projects we propose and the questions we ask. From this perspective, existentialism admits pluralism: 'The totality of the object's verified answers constitutes its truth: its truth, of course, in the light of that project. Other projects would allow other truths to rise up unified with the first ones since the object delivers no truths other than those that are asked of it.'[33]

For Sartre, a commitment to the truth and value of one's own beliefs is essential to authentic human action. And yet, I must realize that the beliefs and values of the other always elude my grasp. Sartre says that there are three levels of analysis: truth as my truth, truth as it is for the other and truth as universal.[34] The first appeals to the basic phenomenology of the ego: the truth is an appearance to a subject. The second opens the intersubjective realm and introduces plurality. The third represents the humanistic goal of reconciling the plurality of first-person experiences of truth. But this goal is limited by the first-person phenomenology of experience. The confines of subjectivity limit my ability to judge the other and his project because I am always somewhat ignorant of the truth as it appears to him. Indeed, I am often ignorant of the truth as it will appear to my future self. This culminates in what Sartre calls 'generosity and liberation': 'Liberation because it gets free of the possibilities of secondary errors; generosity because truth is thus given to the alter ego I will be and to the others by *allowing them to make of it what they will*.'[35] This last claim is essentially a plea for toleration.

Toleration, risk and action

The existential approach described here has a very limited positive content and can only result in a very minimal theory of justice. This approach is *negative*: it negates my assurances about myself, it negates my assurances about the mores and laws of my community and it negates my assurances about my ability to judge the other. The existential approach restrains me by showing me the lack of transparent self-justification of my principles or of the principles of the other. And yet we must have faith in truth and the possibility of mutual understanding. Otherwise our ethical commitments evaporate and our dialogical encounters with others become meaningless. Although existentialism remains open to diversity and is dubious about absolute truth, it does not give up the concrete truth of human existence in a shared world. Indeed, the struggle against dogmatism and totalitarianism is both a struggle against absolute frameworks, which force human freedom into a preset mould, and a struggle against totalitarian denial of concrete human truth. As Camus says: 'We have a right to think that truth with a capital letter is relative. But facts are facts. And whoever says that the sky is blue when it is gray is prostituting words and preparing the way for tyranny.'[36]

Toleration follows as the ground for judgement of others becomes obscure. Often we do not know whether our judgements are justified, just as we do not know whether our practices or the practices of the other are justified. This leads to resistance to our initial impulses in reaction to the other. Of course, one cannot remain inactive just as one cannot tranquilize the judging faculty. We eventually return to activity and to judgement – as we must and as we should. However, when we retain a memory of the moment of transcendence, our activity and judgement become more tolerant, as we realize that to judge is to take a risk. Although we must act and judge, we must recognize that our activities and judgements are the activities of a finite being for whom activity and judgment remain a risk. When I encounter incomprehensible and repugnant behaviour in another, I restrain myself under the recognition that my own behaviours are often not themselves transparently good. Although I must engage the world, this engagement becomes more circumspect, less self-assured and more tolerant when it recognizes itself against a background of finitude and uncertainty. Here in fact is a crucial difference between the atheistic existentialists and theistic existentialists such as Kierkegaard. For Camus, Sartre and Beauvoir, the leap of faith implied in judgement and action remains a risk that cannot be redeemed by a benevolent God.

The critique of totalitarianism and state violence that is found in Camus and Beauvoir is a critique of that form of dogmatic self-certainty that ignores the continued need for self-questioning. Beauvoir says: 'If the fusion of the Commissar and the Yogi were realized there would be a self-criticism in the man of action which would expose to him the ambiguity of his will, thus arresting the imperious drive of his subjectivity and, by the same token, contesting the unconditioned value of the goal.'[37] And Camus says: 'The rebel thus rejects divinity in order to share in the struggles and destiny of all men ... Each tells the other that he is not God.'[38] Such ideas surely call for toleration, even as they risk apathy and indifference. This distinction between toleration and apathy is found in the existential necessity of choice and commitment in a social setting. As Sartre explains: 'The doctrine I am presenting is the very opposite of quietism, since it declares, "there is no reality except in action".'[39] Although existentialism can seem to be solipsistic, individual consciousness is always mediated by the other: 'Thus comprehension is nothing other than my real life; it is the totalizing movement which gathers together my neighbor, myself, and the environment in the synthetic unity of an objectification in process.'[40] Or: 'In order to get any truth about myself, I must have contact with another person.'[41] In this way, toleration and openness to the other are necessary for the development of individual self-consciousness.

However, toleration has its limits. What if the other is attacking me or is injuring others? Clearly, I must act to defend what I perceive as right. And yet self-defence or even war can be undertaken in a tolerant fashion: by resisting the temptation to see war as a clash of absolutes based in a totalizing form of hatred. Camus makes this clear in his 'Letter to a German Friend' where he speaks to the German about the necessity of destroying the German's power: 'I can tell you that at the very moment when we are going to destroy you without pity, we still feel no hatred toward you ... We want to destroy you in your power without mutilating you in your soul.'[42] Even self-defence can be undertaken tolerantly, with the recognition that neither of us is entirely clear to ourselves and both of us are at risk. Although I will certainly defend myself, I will not become vengeful and seek retribution because I recognize that the ignorance that led the other to attack me is not unique to him. We are all ignorant. We are all struggling for light in the midst of darkness. My recognition of the sense of mystery in the other can help me – within limits – to tolerate the other because I recognize that the other, like me, is doing the best he can to make sense of his life. I may believe that he is mistaken in his attempts to make sense of himself, however, I must recognize that the mystery of self cannot be resolved from without. I cannot force an interpretation of self upon the other. Rather, I should tolerantly allow him to struggle with the mystery of his own self, while encouraging him towards self-knowledge. In the same way, I want him to tolerantly encourage me to struggle with my own transcendence.

In this way, existentialism leads towards an ideal of dialogue such as is found in Martin Buber's writings, as discussed in Chapter 3. Since I am focusing on non-theistic existentialists, however, I will cite here Merleau-Ponty who emphasizes that language, as the method of access between individuals, is essentially dialogical and that dialogue opens a shared world of experience: 'In the experience of dialogue, there is constituted between the other person and myself a common ground: my thought and his are interwoven into a single fabric ... We are collaborators for each other in consummate reciprocity. Our perspectives merge into each other, and we co-exist through a common world.'[43] Of course, this idea of consummate reciprocity may be too strong an ideal for mortal beings and it can become repressive when institutionalized. As Beauvoir says: 'One can reveal the world only on a basis revealed by other men. No project can be defined except by its interference with other projects.'[44] The notion of interference is key here. Although dialogue and mutual understanding is our goal, we discover that in opening ourselves to the other, we often develop those negative emotions that toleration asks us to resist. If we recognize finitude and uncertainty and the freedom of the other, perhaps the best we can hope for is toleration on the way towards more genuine dialogue.

Conclusion: dogmatism, silence and toleration

Various forms of dogmatism deny the existential condition. It is important to note that existentialism is not primarily a moral system. Rather, it offers an ontological theory of human existence that is based upon the fact that we are condemned to be free. Thus the form of toleration we find here argues against dogmatism on an ontological and epistemological level. We *should* be tolerant because we *are* free. From the dogmatist's perspective, the content of freedom to be filled out by the truth has been revealed in an ancient text or a charismatic authority. Such an approach to freedom becomes intolerant when the dogmatist claims that the truth is such, that non-believers are wrong, and that questioning authority is not freedom.

Sartre and other existentialists resisted the imposition of social categories upon the freedom of the individual. We see this in Heidegger's discussion of authenticity in opposition to the 'the they'. But Heidegger's discussion makes it look as if the self is enticed by 'the they' into alienating itself by adopting social categories – as if the alienation and intolerance of social being are what he calls 'tempting and tranquilizing'.[45] Unlike Heidegger, Sartre and the French existentialists are closer to Marx in their awareness of the fact that the alienation of social being can be oppressively forced upon us. The idea of race is used, for example, to oppress people by imposing a socially constructed idea upon the free individual. From the position of a Jew under Nazism, to cite a specific example, the oppressive nature of social control becomes apparent because the free individual feels himself forced into a role or category that he did not choose for himself. Oppression is discovered in any social category, which does not respect my freedom:

> Because I am a minor I shall not have this or that privilege. Because I am a Jew I shall be deprived of certain possibilities. Yet I am unable in any way to feel myself as a Jew or as a minor or as a pariah. It is at this point that I can react against these interdictions by declaring that race, for example, is purely and simply a collective fiction, that only individuals exist.[46]

Intolerance is not letting individuals exist in their freedom by refusing to view people as complex projects of self-creation.

When we confront intolerance, then, we must not be naïve: we must use whatever force is necessary to reduce the kinds of threats to freedom found in intolerant dogmatism. We will do our best to educate the other and when this fails, then we will turn – reluctantly – to more extreme measures. Of course, we must be cautious here. But, as noted with regard to Camus' 'Letters to a German Friend', resistance in the name of tolerance, freedom and justice can be forceful while not becoming an intolerant imposition of one more dogmatic absolute.

Although I stated at the outset that I would not attempt to resolve Sartre and Camus' dispute about violence, the dialogue between them is instructive. Sartre's 'Reply to Albert Camus' provides us with an example of a sort of toleration, which I will consider here in conclusion. In this article, Sartre described his break with Camus in terms that show us the problem of individual differences and the ongoing task of toleration. Although Camus and Sartre were friends, Sartre claims, 'Friendship, too, tends to become totalitarian.'[47] This is so, because each friend tends to want the other, narcissistically, to conform to his idea of the good. Unfortunately, the absolute coincidence of interests and ideas usually only happens by means of subtle (and occasionally not-so-subtle) forms of coercion. When this becomes apparent, friendships dissolve and individuals confront each other across their differences. But this does not mean, for Sartre, that friends become enemies. Rather, there is a third possibility, a middle ground, that can best be described as toleration. Sartre's rebuke of Camus and his rejection of Camus' *The Rebel* was vigorous and one might suspect that the switch from friend to enemy had been complete. However, Sartre ends his essay, not with enmity, not with reconciliation: but with toleration: 'I have said what you were for me and what you are now. But whatever you may say or do in return, I refuse to fight you. I hope that our silence will cause this polemic to be forgotten.'[48]

This conclusion is quite different from Camus' conclusion in his 'Letters to a German Friend'. And yet both adhere to an ideal of toleration that is enacted differently depending upon the context. With Camus, we see a reluctant turn to violence in the name of toleration; with Sartre, we see toleration as polemic followed by silence and continued disagreement. Both approaches follow from a commitment to freedom. When freedom is threatened we must fight. But in all other cases, when freedom itself is not in jeopardy, we can agree to disagree. Although we can hope that the confrontation across difference will result in a dialogue that is more than the icy silence Sartre proposes here, at least the silence of toleration is better than the heat and violence of intolerance. Of course silence itself can be intolerant and totalitarian, as Camus notes: 'We suffocate among people who think they are absolutely right, whether in their machines or in their ideas. And for all who can live only in an atmosphere of human dialogue and sociability, this silence is the end of the world.'[49] The hope of dialogue should inspire us to move towards reciprocal freedom and recognition of one another's alterity. But until the utopian moment when we are all able to come together in solidarity, until we are able to overcome our fallibility and eradicate the mystery of human being, toleration serves as an inevitable and useful value for the formation of tragic communities of difference.

Notes

1. Albert Camus, 'Bread and Freedom' in *Resistance, Rebellion, and Death*, New York: Vintage, 1995, p. 90.

2. For a discussion of the dispute between Camus and Sartre, see Germaine Bree, *Camus and Sartre: Crisis and Commitment*, New York: Delacorte Press, 1972.

3. Herbert Marcuse, 'Repressive Tolerance' in Wolff, Moore, and Marcuse (eds) *A Critique of Pure Tolerance*, Boston: Beacon Press, 1969, p. 110.

4. *Ibid.*, p. 107.

5. Slavoj Zizek, 'A Plea for Leninist Intolerance', *Critical Inquiry*, 28, (Winter 2002), p. 558.

6. Theodore Adorno, *Minima Moralia*, London: Verso, 1994, p. 25.

7. See Freud's analysis of Christian morality in *Civilization and its Discontents*, New York: Norton, 1961, pp. 66–9.

8. Maurice Merleau-Ponty, *Humanism and Terror*, Boston: Beacon Press, 1969, p. 188.

9. David E. Cooper, *Existentialism*, Oxford: Basil Blackwell, 1990, chapter 10; also see Thomas C. Anderson, *Sartre's Two Ethics*, Chicago: Open Court Press, 1993, chapter 5.

10. Sartre, *Being and Nothingness*, New York: Washington Square Press, 1956, p. 72.

11. *Ibid.*, p. 76.

12. Camus, *The Rebel*, New York: Vintage Books, 1991, p. 252.

13. Albert Camus, *Neither Victims nor Executioners*, Philadelphia: New Society Publishers, 1986, p. 52.

14. Albert Camus, *The Myth of Sisyphus and Other Essays*, New York: Vintage, 1991.

15. Zygmunt Bauman, *Liquid Modernity*, Cambridge: Polity Press, 2000, p. 34.

16. Søren Kierkegaard, *The Sickness Unto Death*, ed. and trans. Howard V. Hong and Edna H. Hong, Princeton, NJ: Princeton University Press, 1980, p. 13.

17. Friedrich Nietzsche, *The Will to Power*, trans. Walter Kaufmann and R.J. Hollingdale, New York: Vintage Books, 1968, §485.

18. Martin Heidegger, 'What is Metaphysics?' in David Farrell Krell (ed.) *Heidegger: Basic Writings*, San Francisco: Harper San Francisco, 1977.

19. Jean-Paul Sartre, *Being and Nothingness*, trans. Hazel E. Barnes, New York: Washington Square Press, 1956, p. 36.

20. Camus, *The Rebel*, p. 17.

21. *Ibid.*, p. 22.

22. *Ibid.*, p. 252.

23. Simone de Beauvoir, *The Ethics of Ambiguity*, Seacaucus, NJ: The Citadel Press, 1948, p. 14.

24. Sartre, *Truth and Existence*, Chicago: University of Chicago Press, 1992, p. 56.

25. *Ibid.*, p. 66.

26. *Ibid.*, p. 65.

27. Sartre, *Being and Nothingness*, p. 106.

28. Camus, *The Rebel*, p. 304.

29. Sartre, 'The Humanism of Existentialism' in *Essays in Existentialism*, Seacausus, NJ: The Citadel Press, 1977, p. 58.

30. Beauvoir, *The Ethics of Ambiguity*, p. 72.

31. *Ibid.*, p. 133.

32. Sartre, *Truth and Existence*, p. 30.

33. *Ibid.*, p. 23.

34. *Ibid.*, p. 65.

35. *Ibid.*, p. 65.

36. Camus, 'Socialism of the Gallows' in *Resistance, Rebellion, and Death*, New York: Vintage, 1995, p. 168.

37. Beauvoir, *The Ethics of Ambiguity*, p. 154.

38. Camus, *The Rebel*, p. 306.

39. Sartre, 'The Humanism of Existentialism' in *Essays in Existentialism*, p. 47.

40. Sartre, *Search for a Method*, New York: Vintage Books, 1968, p. 155.

41. Sartre, 'The Humanism of Existentialism' in *Essays in Existentialism*, p. 52.

42. Camus, 'Letters to a German Friend' in *Resistance, Rebellion, and Death*, p. 31.

43. Merleau-Ponty, *Phenomenology of Perception*, London: Routledge, 1992, p. 354.

44. Beauvoir, *The Ethics of Ambiguity*, p. 72.

45. Heidegger, *Being and Time*, New York: Harper and Row, 1962, pp. 222–3.

46. Sartre, *Being and Nothingness*, pp. 671–2.

47. Sartre, 'Reply to Albert Camus' in *Situations*, New York: George Braziller, 1965, p. 71.

48. Sartre, 'Reply to Albert Camus' in *Situations*, p. 105.

49. Camus, *Neither Victims nor Executioners*, p. 29.

7

Liberal Toleration

Thus far, I have focused on the virtue of tolerance and have attempted to revive certain neglected resources for understanding this virtue. In this chapter I will shift gears somewhat in order to focus on political toleration in the liberal tradition. The difficulty of liberal toleration is found in its attempt to negotiate the differences between political toleration and a more comprehensive moral ideal. The most prominent recent defender of the ideal of liberal political toleration is John Rawls, who defends toleration from the perspective of a form of public reason in which the conditions for a well-ordered pluralistic society are defined. Rawls explicitly contrasts his notion of public reasonableness with a more substantive or comprehensive view of reason: 'I propose that in public reason comprehensive doctrines of truth or right be replaced by an idea of the politically reasonable addressed to citizens as citizens.'[1] Thus the form of toleration that is derived from a Rawlsian perspective cannot be the same as the sort of tolerance found in the moral traditions I have discussed thus far. In the next chapter I will describe how Rawls' approach has much in common with American pragmatism's attempt to deal with the fact of pluralism. It should be noted that the Rawlsian approach does share in common with the previous traditions the idea that modesty is important: Rawls' idea of public reason is a modest one, which self-consciously avoids making claims about substantive issues. But Rawls is careful to note that this modesty is not full-blown scepticism. He explicitly disavows scepticism and claims that reasonable pluralism follows from the fact that there are 'many difficulties in reaching agreement arising with all kinds of judgement. These difficulties are particularly acute in the case of political judgements in view of the very great complexity of the questions raised, the often impressionistic nature of the evidence, and the severity of the conflict they commonly address.'[2] Ronald Beiner notes this sort of modesty in a critical remark aimed at liberals such as Rawls: 'Philosophers have failed to produce important reflections on moral and political life not for want of ability but because they believed it did not befit the philosopher to pronounce on what is important and essential in human life ... They were persuaded that such "modesty" was appropriate to the philosophical vocation.'[3]

Political liberalism is in fact a modest and pragmatic account of how best to negotiate differences within our pluralistic society. Political liberalism self-consciously avoids substantial claims about the good life, a point that has been made by authors who defend what has come to be known as a communitarian view.[4] Political toleration is about organizing large groups of people based on what Nagel calls 'higher-order impartiality'.[5] But as Nagel and others have indicated, the notion of 'higher-order impartiality' is itself not impartial, which leads to the paradox of toleration. If we tolerate something, it is thought that we must in some way, disapprove of it. Groups or individuals who are merely tolerated will thus rightly feel slighted, especially if they want a more robust sort of recognition within the political community.[6] But the ideal of mutual recognition seems to go beyond toleration towardss a sort of utopian community that is in fact impossible in the real world of actual differences. Toleration is required in the real world in which the possibility of mutual recognition is, in some sense, lacking. The real world contains power differences, majority groups and minority groups: liberal toleration attempts to find ways of negotiating these differences without unduly intervening in the redistribution of power.

The virtue of tolerance described in previous chapters is part of a substantive ethical position that respects autonomy and values difference as a necessary part of the human experience. Such respect for autonomy and difference requires both that we be tolerant of others and that we critically interact with them. Tolerance, as I have discussed it thus far, is not mere neutrality or impartiality because it involves engagement with the other. But political toleration does aim for neutrality or impartiality, in part because political toleration is about the restraint of the coercive power of the state and what Mill called 'the tyranny of prevailing opinion'. Among individuals we can tolerate others while engaging with them in the project of building temporary communities of inquiry. But once individuals join together to form groups and once these groups create institutions of power, the matter is changed. In political situations, neutrality or impartiality is required in the name of fairness. However, power is always an issue, as the group of individuals doing the tolerating have a sort of power that is lacked by members of the groups that are tolerated. Although it would be nice to confine remarks about politics to claims about individuals, at the level of politics individuals are always already members of groups. This indicates part of the problem of political toleration: it is about individuals insofar as they are members of groups, an idea which runs contrary to the moral idea of tolerance that is derived from respect for the autonomy of individuals. In this sense, political life is always ripe for tragedy, as political life requires that individuals be identified in ways that run counter to the idea of individual autonomy.

Some recent authors have attempted to defend a more substantive or comprehensive liberal ideal.[7] Such approaches are reminiscent of the sort of philosophical communities I have described previously. But the problem with these approaches is that they fail to account for the problem of political power in a satisfying way. For this reason, Rawls' version of political liberalism is perhaps preferable as a description of political life. But Rawls' approach fails to offer us hope for the development of more substantive communities. Thus again we are faced with a tragic choice: a substantive liberal community that may be less sensitive to the fact of power or a more political sort of liberal community that will provide us with less opportunity to develop a more substantial sort of community. I think that we would do well to admit this conflict, while admitting that it cannot be adequately reconciled. We need a certain sort of toleration at the level of politics. We need a different sort of tolerance at the level of the local community. Although I do think that political toleration offers the best hope for the development of local communities of tolerance, conflicts and problems will remain.

The main difficulty is that the dialogical method found in the Socratic community can be offensive to those whose moral or religious creeds discourage such dialogue. Local communities of inquiry can ignore such dogmatists by excluding them from the dialogue. But in the political sphere, the problem is to find a way to integrate dogmatists of this sort into the liberal political community and include them in the system of social distributions. Political toleration is required precisely for those who do not share the substantive commitments of liberalism but who wish to coexist with those who do.

Locke's epistemological liberalism

Liberalism is ultimately about the limits of state power. The very idea of a limit to state power is expressed in the concept of 'human right': our rights indicate limits to state intervention. Thus liberals such as Locke articulate most of their arguments using the language of rights. But this language can be vacuous unless it is explained why we have these rights. Locke often talks as if our rights are based in God or in Nature. This can appear to be something of a postulate that cannot be further analysed. But a

further analysis is possible, if we consider what I call the 'epistemological argument', which focuses on the nature of belief and the
importance of inward sincerity (as discussed in Chapter 5).

Before we turn to this directly it is important to note that liberalism is a negative view that is opposed to authoritarian political
ideals. Perhaps the most famous and troubling version of the
authoritarian ideal is found in Plato's *Republic*, where individual
liberty is sacrificed to the authority of the philosopher–king. This
ideal is troubling because it is so central to the Western tradition
of thinking about politics. Moreover, the ideal of Socratic tolerance runs counter to the spirit of Platonic politics. The problem
identified by liberal thinking is that when power is consolidated
in the hands of one man or a ruling clique, it tends to become
intolerant. The liberal goal of limiting intolerant power is thus
linked to ideas about the limits of state power and to institutional mechanisms for diffusing power through a system of checks
and balances.

The example of Plato is important because it lies at the heart of
the Western tradition, which was eventually to develop liberal
political thought. Karl Popper has gone so far as to claim that
Plato was Socrates' 'least faithful disciple' because he betrayed
Socrates' commitment to open inquiry and the open society.[8]
Likewise, John Stuart Mill found the example of Marcus Aurelius,
who persecuted the Christians, a troubling example of the problem of a Platonic approach to politics.[9] The examples of Plato
and Marcus remind us that there is something appealing about
a utopia consisting of a unified society ruled by a wise authority.
At best, the philosopher–king would endeavour to be personally
tolerant, as we saw in our discussion of Marcus. But there is no
guarantee that this sort of personal virtue will lead to a system of
political toleration. A commitment to liberal values will thus have
to sacrifice the Platonic dream in the name of liberty and toleration of diversity. But we must not pretend that this sacrifice is
not a serious loss: there is something deeply appealing about the

Platonic dream of unity and harmony, even though this dream is incompatible with the values that are central to liberalism.

One of the most basic arguments for toleration found in the liberal tradition is epistemological: it is about the nature of belief as well as a claim about the nature of truth. One version of the epistemological argument is found in Locke and another is found in Mill. The epistemological argument has been revisited recently by Ronald Dworkin who phrases it as follows:

> Ethical liberals know that they cannot make other people's lives better by the coercive means that liberal tolerance forbids, because they know that someone's life cannot be improved against his steady conviction that it has not been. Even if they think someone's life would be better if he changed his convictions, they know they cannot make it better unless he does change them, and in the right way.[10]

The point here is ultimately about the psychology of belief. It is the claim that rational beings cannot be coerced into believing that something is true. More broadly, free individuals cannot be coerced into believing their lives are good or bad.

This epistemological argument shows us the limit of the Platonic model. The idea, as expressed by Plato in the *Republic*, that harmony can be created by the rule of the philosopher–king is false, from this perspective. Plato claims that the wisdom of the philosopher–king will translate downward throughout the levels of society, establishing unity and justice. But the Lockean position holds that there can be no such downward translation. Rather, individuals must come to know the truth for themselves. The idea of the 'noble lie' simply will not work to produce harmony because individuals will demand the right to discover and believe the truth for themselves.

Toleration is often confused with relativism. So we must be careful to point out that this claim about the formation of genuine

belief is not a sort of relativism that says that people believe different things and are entitled to these differences because there is no
such thing as justified true belief.[11] The point of claiming that we
ought to tolerate others is itself not relative and is intended to be a
claim of truth: since it is true that coercion cannot produce genuine true belief, it is true that we ought to tolerate others with whom
we disagree. Rather than being a variety of relativism, this form of
toleration starts from a fundamental claim about the nature of
human belief. For individuals to genuinely believe the truth, they
must believe it because it is true, and not because they are afraid of
punishment, etc. In other words, as developed in Chapter 5,
inward sincerity is the key to belief. This modern idea does go
back to Plato, who used it to argue that only philosophers could
know the truth. Unfortunately, Plato conjoined this with the
claim that it would be permissible for philosophers to coerce and
even lie to those who were incapable of knowing the truth in this
way. Liberals are much more optimistic and egalitarian about
human capacity. They believe that most human beings are
capable of knowing the truth. Thus liberals are not willing to allow
coercion with regard to belief because liberals hold that coercion
cannot produce genuine belief.

This idea is most prominent in Locke's argument for toleration, although we also saw it in Spinoza, as discussed briefly in
Chapter 5. Locke is worried about the human tendency to use violence in the name of irrationality.[12] Not only is violence joined to
political authority dangerous, but it is also irrational because of
the way in which belief functions. Locke argues that the civil and
ecclesiastical authorities ought to tolerate diversity of belief
because one cannot *force* another human being to have faith. This
is true, in part, because belief is, in a sense, not subject to the will:
for genuine beliefs, we must use reason – we cannot simply employ
will to believe something that our reasoning faculty finds to be
false. Toleration is required because the beliefs of others are not,
ultimately, in our control. Thus Locke's account is related, at

least in spirit, to the Stoic idea that we should learn to forbear those things which are not in our control.

Moreover, Locke holds that truth will win out, if reason were only permitted to do its work: 'For the truth certainly would do well enough if she were left to shift for herself ... She is not taught by laws, nor has she any need of force to procure her entrance into the minds of men.' Locke concludes: 'Anyone may employ as many exhortations and arguments as he please. But all force and compulsion are to be forborne.' This is so because, 'every man has the supreme and absolute authority of judging for himself.'[13]

The epistemological claim is the focal point of Jeremy Waldron's critique of Locke's account of tolerance. Waldron claims that Locke's argument is weak because it is a false assumption that beliefs cannot be coerced. With regard to the question of whether beliefs can be coerced, I remain agnostic at this point, although I must admit that Waldron has a point. We often believe things quite sincerely without any good reason whatsoever – this was the problem that Plato saw and the reason he distinguished philosophers as the few who believed for good reasons. The more crucial point is found in Waldron's conclusion that Locke's concern with combating the supposed epistemological problem of intolerance leaves Locke unable or unwilling to tell us why intolerance is 'wrong'.[14] The point here is that the epistemological argument is too weak to provide a moral limitation on coercion. Even though coercion cannot produce genuine belief, an intolerant regime may not be interested in producing genuine belief. It may simply be interested in guaranteeing conformity. Waldron's point is important. The epistemological critique is useful only if one is committed to the claim that a genuine belief in the truth is an important political or moral value. Not only is it impractical to impose belief upon others, but liberals also tend to believe that we ought to value genuine commitment over mere conformity.

Now, however, supposing Waldron is correct and beliefs can be coerced, the moral question still remains: is it right for a liberal state to coerce its people into certain beliefs? The point here is a bit subtler. Even though it might be possible to coerce a person to believe something, the question is whether this is good. One of the hallmarks of the liberal tradition is the idea that liberty *should* not be violated. Locke's epistemological argument was that such liberty *could not* practically be violated. The more substantive moral point is that such liberty *should not* be violated.

Locke appeals to Christianity as a foundation for toleration. The idea that rational beings must believe for the right reasons is, from Locke's perspective, the foundation of the Christian message. A belief in Christ cannot be coerced or compelled. Rather, it must be a belief that is held for the right reasons, namely out of a sincere belief that it is true. Locke states: 'The toleration of those that differ from others in matters of religion is so agreeable to the Gospel of Jesus Christ and to the genuine reason of mankind, that it seems monstrous for men to be so blind as not to perceive the necessity and advantage of it in so clear a light.'[15] His primary focus with regard to toleration is toleration of diverse Christian denominations in light of the remaining mysteries of Christian doctrine.[16] But it is easy to see that this idea could be expanded to include other religions.

The epistemological approach to toleration argues against forcing non-believers to believe. But this poses problem for religious believers who feel compelled to make others believe the truth. If the epistemological argument is plausible, then the state (and other authorities) ought to refrain from attempting to create communities of belief. But this leaves real communities of belief without access to public means of disseminating their faiths. And this will be a troubling outcome for religious communities that are convinced that their message is essential for the eternal salvation of people's souls. The epistemological argument is quite closely linked to the Socratic ideal of a community of inquiry: individuals must develop genuine beliefs for themselves by way of tolerant dialogue. But the Socratic ideal will be rejected by some religious believers. Such religious believers may thus feel that the tolerant state is not impartial; but that it, rather, promotes an anti-religious agenda based upon its epistemological assumptions.

Mill and the moral affirmation of diversity

Locke's account is limited because of its own religious foundations: Locke would not tolerate atheists, for example. A more robust moral limitation on the coercive power of the state is found in something like Mill's account, which argues in favour of diversity and liberty. Thus Mill's account, by linking the epistemological concern with a normative claim about the value of diversity as such, provides a more robust theory of toleration. Nonetheless, the epistemological question remains crucial because a sovereign self needs access to the truth in order to be able to be rationally responsible. Although Locke does not link the epistemological question to the moral question of substantive liberty in this way, I agree with Susan Mendus who claims that something like Locke's epistemological account provides the most stable ground for toleration.[17] While I agree with the epistemological argument, especially as it applies to Socratic communities of inquiry, it is problematic when applied at the level of politics, as mentioned above.

Mill's celebration of diversity may seem even more troubling to those committed to religious ideals or other more substantial conceptions of the good life. Mill's idea of diversity may seem to be a celebration of relativism. If so, it would also run counter to the epistemological ideal of the Socratic community: that tolerance is a useful virtue as we pursue truth. However, Mill is not a relativist in this way. Mill's account of liberty is also based in part on the epistemological problem articulated by Locke.

Mill's argument follows from certain basic assumptions about individuals.

1   Each individual has a will of his (or her) own.
2   Individuals are generally better off when not compelled to 'do better'.
3   Each individual knows his (or her) own best good.
4   Each individual is motivated to attain his own good and to not act contrary to his own best interests.
5   Self-regarding thought and activity can be distinguished from its effects upon others.

It is clear that some of these claims (e.g., no. 3) are linked to the epistemological approach. Of course, Mill admits that it is possible for individuals to be mistaken about their own best good. Thus Mill concludes that critical engagement is necessary for us. Mill concludes his introduction of the liberty principle with the following: 'There are good reasons for remonstrating with him, or reasoning with him, or persuading him, or entreating him, but not for compelling him, or visiting him with any evil in case he do otherwise.'[18] Criticism is necessary, because although the individual is ultimately his own best judge, individuals need criticism in order to discover what their own good might be. Mill aims for an education that goes beyond coercion towards genuine rational discourse aimed at producing sincere conviction.[19]

Mill's argument for diversity is thus not an argument for relativism. Rather, Mill remains interested in truth and in the Socratic process of dialogical education. Indeed, this helps explain his idea in *Utilitarianism*, that there are higher and lower forms of happiness.[20] It might seem that Mill's idea of a moral hierarchy of happiness (that the happiness of Socrates is better than the happiness of the fool or the pig) is intolerant. However, Mill's idea of toleration is linked to his fallibilism, his empiricism and to the desire to maintain an open argument about this. Ultimately this is an epistemological claim. Mill thinks that Socrates will know that his happiness is better because he has experienced both sides. But Mill recognizes that there will be those who have not yet experienced both sides. Education is the process of opening people to possibilities for experience. We expose them to the Socratic pleasures. But we allow them to make up their own mind about which pleasures are better for them. And it is quite possible – even if unlikely – that different people will reach different conclusions about the hierarchy of happiness. Thus we must remain tolerant even as we disagree. Nonetheless, Mill's faith is that the tolerant and critical dialogue that will ensue will be good for all of us.[21]

Mill defends a view of knowledge that requires strong and vigorous contestation. He concludes that 'no one's opinions deserve the name of knowledge, except so far as he has either had forced upon him by others, or gone through of himself, the same mental process which would have been required of him in carrying on an active controversy with opponents'.[22] In Chapter 2 of *On Liberty*, in his defence of freedom of thought, Mill makes the following crucial points with regard to knowledge and freedom of thought:

1 Silenced opinions may be true. To assume they are not is to assume that we are *infallible*.
2 Silenced opinions may be false – but even false opinions contain valid points of *contention*. We require to hear and respond to even false opinions in order to know the whole of truth.
3 Even if we do know the truth, we must know this in the fullest sense of the term: we must be able to *defend it* against all vigorous opposition.
4 Truth that is not *vigorously contested* becomes mere superstition. It may thus crumble before even weak opposition and will not be heartily believed or defended.

Thus Mill's defence of toleration is based upon the belief that through toleration, truth will result. This is the basic idea of a philosophical community devoted to the discovery of truth through dialectic. Mill himself emphasizes that what he has in mind is something quite similar to the Socratic dialectic.[23] Mill expands this into the social and political realm and thus holds out the hope that a tolerant society might be better able to discover the truth. However, since we are fallible, this remains a mere hope. Toleration is required because we do not yet possess the truth and we must respect the fact that different individuals will have different approaches to the truth and will arrive at the truth at their own pace. As Mill concludes: 'Truth, in the great practical concerns of life, is so much a question of the reconciling and combining of opposites, that very few have minds sufficiently capacious and impartial to make the adjustments with an approach to correctness, and it has to be made by the rough process of a struggle between combatants fighting under hostile banners.'[24] We can see, then, that Mill adopts a dialogical view of knowledge and that he wants to encourage diversity so as to foster a stronger dialogue leading to a more complex and robust truth. This idea leads to a decidedly antinomian conclusion: that it may be in the interest of truth to foster diversity, even by actively supporting those with whom we disagree. Mill follows the previously quoted sentence with the following: 'On any of the great open questions if either of the two opinions has a better claim than the other, not merely to be tolerated, but to be encouraged and countenanced, it is the one which happens at the particular time and place to be in a minority.'[25] This conclusion leads to the idea that political power should actively support minority views, an idea that will be vigorously rejected by those who are not as liberal as Mill. An obvious argument against this has been articulated by those who resist efforts to use their tax money or student fees to support groups with whom they disagree in an effort to level the playing field and create an open forum of ideas, as we shall see subsequently.

Toleration, multiculturalism and the open forum of ideas

Mill indicates that a truly tolerant political regime might actually go so far as to support voices with whom the majority disagrees. Of course, this cannot mean that a genuine liberal regime would actively support voices that subvert the liberal democratic ideal; this would be a reiteration of the paradox of toleration. A tolerant society need not actively encourage dogmatic anti-liberals. Mill's idea of supporting dissent does not mean that we must give active support to those voices that deliberately advocate abolishing dissent. What is at issue here is not support for anti-liberal voices, but support for the plurality of voices that disagree about a wide variety of substantive issues. Thus we might use tax money or student fees to support groups that have historically been marginalized such as gays and lesbians, or minority religions such as Islam, or groups dedicated to reproductive rights. This approach may be offensive to other groups who are opposed to having their resources redistributed to groups with whom they disagree.

Mill's conclusion might be that liberal regimes should actively support a variety of dissenting voices without, however, actively supporting anti-liberal voices that advocate the abolition of dissent. The idea of active support of minority groups has been discussed under general rubrics such as 'group rights', 'preservation of cultures', 'the politics of difference' or 'multiculturalism'. The point is that a liberal regime might go out of its way to help an embattled minority group to survive.[26] But with this idea of active support, we go somewhat beyond toleration.

When private individuals tolerate those whose morality they disagree with, they allow what they perceive to be immoral to continue to exist, as long as there is no concrete harm to others that result from this toleration. But it is odd to demand that individuals should go beyond mere tolerance towards active support of what they perceive as 'immorality' in pursuit of an open forum of ideas.

We have noted that in the Socratic community, tolerance need not be indifferent or uncritical. Even Mill admits that we can use speech to educate, admonish and exhort. However, when political institutions tolerate diversity and redistribute resources so as to encourage diversity, there can be strange results that are offensive to groups dedicated to certain comprehensive schemes. In the name of political toleration, political institutions should go to great lengths to refrain from actively criticizing the activities of individuals because critical speech articulated by political power is coercive. But coercion also results when, in the name of toleration, political power actively redistributes resources in a way that violates some citizens' substantive moral commitments.

When one considers the plight of certain marginalized groups and when one bears in mind the power of what Mill called the tyranny of prevailing opinion, it might seem justified for political power to actively support minority groups that are embattled and impoverished by the dominant culture. But if one is sceptical about state coercion, it will be difficult to make this argument, since it would involve taking resources from some individuals and redistributing them to others who are members of the minority group. Indeed, the anarchist/libertarian argument should be one that is familiar to such advocates of multiculturalism, since it is state power that often results in the impoverishment and oppression of minority cultures. The difficulty is how to remedy this problem: through more state intervention, which will result in more coercion and oppression, or through the dissolution of state power. This is a complicated and vexing issue that lies at the heart of much of the discussion about multiculturalism, liberalism and libertarianism. I do not have the space here to adequately discuss this issue further, other than to conclude that this points us again to the tragic nature of political power: decisions made in the name of toleration can themselves appear to be intolerant.

Conclusion

Both Mill and Locke offer arguments for toleration that go beyond the self-consciously limited 'political' arguments of Rawls. Locke focuses on the nature of belief. And Mill aims at maximizing the happiness of all individuals in society. These theories are more substantial than Rawls' explicitly political conception of toleration. For Mill, toleration is good because a society that is tolerant will be one in which individual happiness is maximized by allowing individuals to pursue whatever it is that makes them happy, within limits established out of respect for the happiness of others. Of course, it remains an open question whether individuals actually want the freedom and toleration that Mill wants to give them. And this marks the limit of Mill's approach. It is possible to imagine an intolerant and illiberal society in which most of the individuals are happy. We see this, in fact, everyday in the way in which people flee from freedom to join cults, gangs and other illiberal organizations. Indeed, the idea of an 'escape from freedom' was a recurrent theme of existentialists, critical theorists and psychoanalysts in the twentieth century. For Erich Fromm, who wrote a book with the title *Escape from Freedom*, the problem was that in contemporary mass society, individuality means nothing other than 'insignificance and powerlessness'.[27] Thus individuals turn to intolerant ideologies and institutions in order to feel a sense of belonging, permanence, stability and community.[28] From Mill's perspective, we would have to explain away this phenomenon by claiming that, although individuals who voluntarily give up their liberty to join intolerant organizations claim they are happy, they are not really as happy as they could be. As we saw, the existentialist approach is to claim that it is the responsibility of individuals to reconcile themselves to their freedom.[29] Individuals who give up their liberty in hope of obtaining self-actualization through conformity are self-deluded and will ultimately be unsuccessful.

Such a critique of those who would willingly submit to an illiberal regime assumes a normative view of human being. It claims that human beings *ought* to want liberty, *ought* to be responsible for themselves, *ought* to learn to deal with their own insignificance and powerlessness and that, in short, human beings *ought* to become enlightened, reasonable adults. I take it that this is what Mill means when he states, 'over himself, over his own body and mind, the individual is sovereign'.[30] This is not merely a description of the way in which governmental interference violates individuality; it is also a normative claim to the effect that *individuals ought to be responsible for themselves*. And this explains why Mill follows this sentence with the infamous paragraph in which he says that it is justifiable to interfere in the lives of children and barbarians. Only individuals who are capable of ruling themselves are protected by the liberty principle.

In this way, liberals believe that liberty is good and that it is something both that individuals do want and that they should want. This ideal thus assumes a substantive view of what a good human life should be. In this way, liberalism is not merely a neutral theory of the state. Rather it is a theory of the way in which human flourishing should occur. A tolerant state is good because it allows individuals to conduct their own experiments in living in order to discover what is good for them. Said differently, liberals believe that it is good for individuals to be sovereign, responsible and free. Thus those who worry that the idea of neutrality is not itself neutral can rightly critique those who, like Rawls, postulate the principles of toleration as a pragmatically negotiated compromise (as explained in the next chapter). Of course the ideal of a limited state is not itself neutral. Liberal neutrality claims that restrained political power is good. The challenge of political liberalism is to find pragmatically agreed upon common ground for groups who do not accept this substantive account.

It should be noted, however, that the ideal of a limited state is one among several political ideals, as mentioned above. These other ideals offer us genuine goods, such as security or substantial equality. Thus the choice of liberalism is a tragic one: liberals choose liberty and chose to sacrifice these other goods. A liberalism that does not admit the tragic character of the choice of ideals is not being honest. Isaiah Berlin is a useful source for this tragic view. He admits the allure of alternatives to liberalism in what he calls 'positive liberty'.[31] And he admits in his essay on John Stuart Mill that there is often a high price to pay for the 'great boon' of freedom.[32]

Substantive liberals such as Locke and Mill view state neutrality as good because they believe that human beings should be encouraged to be responsible for their own freedom. But this view is not without its risks, uncertainties and sacrifices. And, indeed, it may be very hard to sustain the substantive moral ideals of autonomy and tolerance within the diversity of our contemporary societies, which is why something like Rawls' more pragmatic account remains important.

Notes

1. John Rawls, 'The Idea of Public Reason Revisited' in *The Law of Peoples*, Cambridge, MA: Harvard University Press, 1999, p. 132. Also see John Rawls, *Political Liberalism*, New York: Columbia University Press, 1995.

2. John Rawls, *Justice as Fairness: A Restatement*, Cambridge, MA: Harvard University Press, 2001, p. 36. Also see *A Theory of Justice*, Cambridge, MA: Harvard University Press, 1971, §34.

3. Ronald Beiner, *What's the Matter with Liberalism?*, Berkeley, CA: University of California Press, 1992, p. 2.

4. See Michael Sandel, *Liberalism and the Limits of Justice*, Cambridge: Cambridge University Press, 1982; or Alasdair MacIntyre, *After Virtue*, Notre Dame, IN: University of Notre Dame Press, 1981.

5. Thomas Nagel, *Equality and Partiality*, Oxford: Oxford University Press, 1991, chapter 14.

6. For a recent discussion of recognition see Anna Elisabetta Galeotti, *Toleration as Recognition*, Cambridge: Cambridge University Press, 2002.

7. Hans Oberdiek, *Tolerance: Between Forbearance and Acceptance*, Lanham, MD: Rowman and Littlefield, 2001; or Kok-Chor Tan, *Toleration, Diversity, and Global Justice*, University Park, PA: Pennsylvania State University Press, 2000, p. 66.

8. Karl Popper, *The Open Society and its Enemies*, Princeton, NJ: Princeton University Press, 1971, 1:194.

9. John Stuart Mill, 'On Liberty' in *On Liberty and Other Essays*, Oxford: Oxford World Classics, 1998, p. 31.

10. Ronald Dworkin, *Sovereign Virtue*, Cambridge, MA: Harvard University Press, 2000, p. 283.

11. Dworkin, for example, has argued vigorously against relativism in 'Objectivity and Truth: You'd Better Believe It', *Philosophy and Public Affairs*, 25:2, Spring 1996.

12. See Ingrid Creppell, 'Locke on Toleration', *Political Theory*, 24:2, 1996, pp. 200–40.

13. John Locke, *Letter Concerning Tolerance* in Steven M. Cahn (ed.) *Classics of Modern Political Theory*, New York: Oxford University Press, 1997, p. 310.

14. Jeremy Waldron, 'Locke: Toleration and the Rationality of Persecution' in John Horton and Susan Mendus (eds) *John Locke: A Letter Concerning Toleration in Focus*, London: Routledge, 1991. For a reply to Waldron that focuses, in part, on the epistemology of belief see Susan Mendus, 'Locke: Toleration, Morality, and Rationality' in John Horton and Susan Mendus (eds) *John Locke: A Lettter Concerning Toleration in Focus*; and Susan Mendus, *Toleration and the Limits of Liberalism*, Atlantic Highlands, NJ: Humanities Press International, 1989, chapter 2.

15. Locke, *Letter Concerning Tolerance*, p. 294.

16. *Ibid.*, pp. 317–19.

17. Susan Mendus, *Toleration and the Limits of Liberalism*, pp. 37–8, 42–3.

18. Mill, *On Liberty*, p. 14.

19. Mill, *ibid.*, p. 84.

20. Mill, *Utilitarianism*, in *On Liberty*, chapter 2.

21. See Isaiah Berlin, 'John Stuart Mill and the Ends of Life' in *Four Essays on Liberty*, Oxford: Oxford University Press, 1969, p. 184.

22. Mill, *On Liberty*, p. 51.

23. *Ibid.*, p. 50.

24. *Ibid.*, p. 54.

25. *Ibid.*

26. See the essays in Gutmann and Taylor (eds) *Multiculturalism*, Princeton, NJ: Princeton University Press, 1994; Iris Marion Young, *Justice*

and the Politics of Difference, Princeton, NJ: Princeton University Press, 1990; and essays by Nancy Fraser, Iris Marion Young and Lawrence Blum in Cynthia Willett (ed.) *Theorizing Multiculturalism*, Oxford: Blackwell, 1998.

27. Erich Fromm, *Escape from Freedom*, New York: Avon Books, 1969, p. 266.
28. Cf. Hannah Arendt's analysis of the way in which the isolation and anomie of mass society lead to totalitarianism in Arendt, *The Origins of Totalitarianism*, New York: Harcourt Brace and Co., 1975, chapter 10.
29. Jeffrey Reiman has noticed the link between substantive liberalism and twentieth-century existentialism (Jeffrey Reiman, *Critical Moral Liberalism*, Lanham, MD: Rowman and Littlefield, 1997).
30. Mill, *On Liberty*, p. 14.
31. Isaiah Berlin, 'Two Concepts of Liberty' in *Four Essays on Liberty*.
32. Isaiah Berlin, *Four Essays on Liberty*, p. 187.

8

Liberalism and Pragmatism

Political toleration is a pragmatic response to the practical need to co-exist with others who have different conceptions of the good. Political toleration develops out of the recognition that, in practice, diversity cannot be eradicated by either philosophical argument or political force. Historically, political toleration is part of a reaction to the totalitarian horrors of those 'final solutions' that have sought to eliminate toleration. We no longer believe that it is practically possible to unify human life under one concept or idea. Political toleration is thus a pragmatic reaction to the concrete fact that diversity exists. In this chapter, I will consider recent discussions of both political toleration and pragmatism in order to show that there is broad agreement among those who explicitly affiliate themselves with American pragmatism and those who are more concerned with the political question of toleration. In particular, I will argue that two of the more prominent recent advocates of political toleration and pluralism, John Rawls and Michael Walzer, argue for toleration on pragmatic grounds.

The fact of diversity

Diversity is the fact of the matter for us today: the world consists of different people with their own ideas of the good. The fact of diversity leads to the practical demand that we tolerate it. Most recent discussions of pluralism reach toleration by way of pragmatic arguments. Karl-Otto Apel argues, for example, that 'we have no other choice in our day than to pursue a cosmopolitan legal order based on political federalism and ethno-religious multiculturalism in the sense of respecting and even supporting a variety of value traditions'.[1] The necessity expressed in Apel's claim ('we have no other choice') is a pragmatic necessity: given the practical goal of peaceful coexistence and the fact of diversity, tolerance is required. Other recent discussions of toleration also make this clear. Even though Bernard Williams argues that toleration is a paradoxical demand to tolerate the intolerable, he views it as a pragmatic political necessity. For Williams, whatever hope there is for toleration lies in the growth of 'international commercial society' together with a practical recognition of the 'manifest harms generated by intolerance'.[2] The problem is, of course, that the idea of manifest harm is itself subject to a plurality of interpretations. Williams admits that there may be no final resolution for the on-going task of toleration because toleration will continually confront intolerance. Williams then concludes that the project of toleration is a practical task continually limited or defined by 'Hobbesian reminders' as the tolerant encounter the intolerant in a world of power politics. The point of these discussions is that toleration results from a pragmatic need and is subject to on-going pragmatic conditions. Toleration is not a metaphysical idea but a continual practical necessity for those of us confronted with the fact of diversity.[3]

Pluralism and toleration are ideas that are dear to the heart of American pragmatists. These ideas stem from pragmatism's self-conscious modesty about our ability to make absolute judgements about the good of human life. Pragmatism also recognizes the basic fact of diversity. As William James noted in his essay 'On a Certain Blindness in Human Beings', although we tend to think that our own view of the world is the only right one, we often find that we simply do not properly understand the point of view of those others whom we might be inclined to criticize. And as James' examples in this essay indicate, we will continue to encounter diversity of ways of life. If we recognize this fact, we reach a tolerant conclusion.[4] James recognizes that the fact of diversity requires toleration.

As is fitting, however, the idea of pluralism at the heart of pragmatism is not a simple one about which there is agreement, even among avowed pragmatists. Richard Rorty draws from James a radical conclusion that tends towards individualism and relativism.[5] As we shall see, John Lachs attempts to walk the line between relativism and absolutism by clarifying a tolerant ideal of pluralism. This struggle is represented, in fact, in the works of Dewey. Dewey discusses toleration in many different places and many different contexts. His conclusions are often caught up in a struggle between, on the one hand, the recognition of the importance of liberty and toleration and, on the other, the recognition of the need for community and integrated social intelligence. Dewey notes explicitly that political toleration and political individualism developed from out of religious toleration and moral individualism.[6] And yet he struggled with the idea of toleration in its social, cultural and political ramifications. We see this in his arguments against radical individualism of the kind envisioned by laissez-faire liberalism.[7] He celebrates Mill's laissez-faire spirit, for example, in 'Liberalism and Social Action'. And yet in that same work he worries that individualism leads to a dissolution of the public sphere and a lack of social intelligence. Rather than private irony of the sort advocated by Rorty, Dewey thinks we need toleration to be embodied in a robust public sphere of intelligent social cooperation. Indeed, Dewey sees this struggle in Mill's own thinking as the tension between Mill's views about liberty and his Benthamite concern for social organization.[8] Dewey's conclusion about toleration is a negative one that views toleration as the pragmatic recognition that the violence of past political struggles has been fruitless: 'Toleration in matters of judgement and belief is largely a negative matter. We agree to leave one another alone (within limits) more from recognition of evil consequences which have resulted from the opposite course rather than from any profound belief in its positive social beneficence.'[9]

Dewey's idea of toleration is thus connected with an idea about the tragic nature of community. Toleration, as a pragmatic idea, is a useful political expedient for dealing with the fact of diversity in the contemporary world. Such a pragmatic response is needed because we cannot support toleration with metaphysical or moral theories since the fact of diversity indicates that there will be continued disagreement about such theories. The pragmatic point is that what is required is not certainty about the metaphysics of human being but a practical recognition of the fact of diversity and of the basic human need for free and peaceful coexistence. But we arrive at toleration because of our failure to create more robust or organic communities. Dewey's diagnosis of the problem of what he calls 'the lost individual' shows us the predicament we are in: 'Individuals vibrate between a past that is intellectually too empty to give stability and a present that is too diversely crowded and chaotic to afford balance or direction to ideas or emotion.'[10] The choice that we make to celebrate diversity is thus a choice that comes with certain costs in terms of instability and chaos. But American philosophers since Emerson have been willing to take this risk and accept these costs in the name of respect for individuality.[11]

Pluralism and relativism: Rawls and Walzer

Toleration and pluralism can easily devolve into the chaos of full-blown relativism.[12] I will argue here that this is not the case. The difference between pluralism and relativism can be fleshed out by considering the difference between Rawls and Walzer. The claim that grounds toleration is that there are plural possibilities for the good. This position has been discussed extensively by Rawls and his critics. In *Theory of Justice*, Rawls says that the idea of justice as fairness sets limits but does not 'try to evaluate the relative merits of different conceptions of the good'; this is because he assumes that 'the plurality of distinct persons with separate systems of ends is an essential feature of human societies'.[13] Rawls' goal is to recognize the fact of diversity and still come up with one set of distributive principles. He does this by way of the heuristic devices of 'the original position' and 'the veil of ignorance'; these are thought experiments that help us to imagine the ideal conditions for deciding about the nature of justice. In his later work, Rawls clarifies his approach by insisting that the principles of justice are political and not moral principles. They are based upon what he calls 'the fact of reasonable pluralism'.[14] This fact must be recognized as we try to establish, practically, a well-ordered society with an overlapping consensus. In recognizing reasonable pluralism, Rawls says:

> Only ideologues and visionaries fail to experience deep conflicts of political values and conflicts between these and nonpolitical values. Profound and long-lasting controversies set the stage for the idea of reasonable justification as a practical and not as an epistemological problem. We turn to political philosophy when our shared political understandings, as Walzer might say, break down and equally when we are torn within ourselves.[15]

The demand for political toleration comes from the fact that conflicting comprehensive doctrines can each be justified as reasonable according to the standards internal to them. This leaves us with the conflicts of reasonable pluralism: each of the conflicting comprehensive doctrines is reasonable on its own terms and to the extent that it recognizes the reasonableness of other comprehensive doctrines. Thus, for Rawls cooperation between reasonable comprehensive doctrines is a practical political task. Rawls thinks the state should refrain from entering into a discussion of which comprehensive doctrine is better morally, epistemologically or metaphysically because a state confronted with the fact of diversity should remain neutral or impartial.[16] By defining this as a *political* task, Rawls wants to distance his account of reasonable pluralism from anything like philosophical scepticism. It is a pragmatic political theory, not a moral theory.[17] In this way Rawls resolves the problem of pluralism in a pragmatic fashion that hearkens back to Locke: since we cannot in practice force individuals to agree about philosophical truths, we should tolerate diversity at the political level. Rawls does hold that there is a best political arrangement, even if the truth about the best political arrangement is arrived at by way of pragmatic concerns for what works politically in light of the fact of diversity.[18]

As seen in the above quote from *Political Liberalism*, Rawls understands himself to be in dialogue with Walzer. Walzer takes pluralism somewhat further than Rawls in claiming that there is a plurality of distributive principles: 'the principles of justice are themselves pluralistic in form'.[19] Unlike Rawls who wants to claim that all reasonable participants in the original position should arrive at the two principles of justice, Walzer wants to admit that differing social or historical milieus could produce different distributive principles. The problem for Walzer is to prevent this pluralism from slipping into relativism. Unfortunately, I am not sure that he is able to prevent this slide. In the final chapter of *Spheres of Justice*, Walzer describes the way in which what he calls 'relativism' follows from the 'non-relative' definition of justice: 'Justice is relative to social meanings. Indeed, the relativity of justice follows from the classic non-relative definition, giving each person his due.'[20] In his more recent essay, *On Toleration*, Walzer explicitly states: 'The idea that our choices are not determined by a single universal principle (or an interconnected set of principles) and that the right choice here might not be similarly right there is, strictly speaking, a relativist idea.'[21] He concludes: 'But I am not advocating an unconstrained relativism, for no arrangement, and no feature of an arrangement, is a moral option unless it provides for some version of peaceful coexistence (and thereby upholds basic human rights)'.[22]

The difficulty is that if Walzer is sincere about his relativism, then there is really no reason for us to accept the tolerant democratic limits he proposes. If it is all relative, then there are no non-relative reasons for us to accept the constraints he wants to impose upon political power. Rather, Walzer should argue that there is at least one non-relative value – that of toleration and peaceful coexistence – even if this is merely pragmatically justified by the concrete historical need for peaceful coexistence among those who cannot arrive at consensus about their views of the good. Each of the diverse members of a pluralistic society agrees to tolerate the other because we agree that genuine unity cannot be coerced and we want to cooperate as best we can. Indeed, this seems to be the gist of Walzer's idea of complex equality: each sphere of social good should be autonomous and not tyrannically dominate other spheres while ensuring cooperation among the spheres. Nonetheless, Walzer's flirtation with relativism leaves his discussion of toleration a bit muddy.[23]

Rawls, unlike Walzer, defends a set of explicitly non-relative principles within which diversity can be supported. Even though they are political, the principles of justice are not relative. Rawls explains this by claiming that pluralism must be 'reasonable'. This means that individuals who tolerate one another must at least admit that they each have good reasons for believing their beliefs even while they disagree. In his discussion of the idea of the reasonable, Rawls proposes that reasonable individuals should: 1) be willing to propose and discuss ideas with one another; 2) be willing to reciprocate with one another; and 3) be willing to accept differences among what Rawls calls 'the burdens of judgement'. This last claim means that reasonable persons should be willing to recognize that the criteria for making sound judgements may be indeterminate and complex enough to lead to a plurality of judgements that could each be called sound. As evidence for this he offers, for example, the fact of differences among what we take to be evidence, differences among our normative values and the weight we will give to evidence, the vagueness of our terms and the very basic fact of conflicting values even within the life of an individual.[24] *Despite* all of this indeterminacy and diversity, Rawls claims that we will be able to recognize one another as reasonable and that reasonable persons will be able to come to agreement about basic political principles which will allow for cooperation. *Because* of all of this indeterminacy and diversity, Rawls argues that reasonable persons will want these principles of cooperation to be tolerant of difference.

The problem for Walzer is that he has overzealously confused pluralism with relativism. Relativism holds that all standards of value are contained entirely within a cultural or historical con-text – or worse, that they are individual matters of opinion and taste. Pluralism, if it is not to become relativism, is the idea that there are various ways in which we may pursue the good; but also that it is possible to say of any of these that it is good according to some non-relative standard. In other words, according to plural-ism, each of the variety of ways we might pursue the good can still be described as good without radically changing the meaning of the term 'good'. Or as Rawls says, each of the ways in which reasonable persons disagree can still be called 'reasonable'. This idea stretches back to Aristotle and his discussion of the way in which virtue consists in the mean 'relative to us'.[25] Although there is one proper mean between the extremes of vice, the proper mean varies for each individual. The proper amount of food for Milo the wrestler will be different from the proper amount of food for me. This does not mean, however, that the concept of a 'proper amount of food' is not definable in non-relative terms. This pluralistic idea lies behind Walzer's misguided claims about relativism. He admits that there is one standard of justice, namely 'giving each his due', although this principle will result in different distributions for different people depending upon their needs and circumstance.

This, however, is not relativism, for it does not deny that there is a standard. It merely states that the standard itself results in differential distributions. This idea is better described as pluralism.

Rawls, Rorty and pragmatism

Toleration results from a pragmatic response to diversity. Although Walzer and Rawls do not, to my knowledge, appeal explicitly to the ideas of American pragmatist philosophers, their accounts beg for interpretation from this perspective. For example, several of Rawl's 'pragmatic' ideas include: the definition of his project as *political* liberalism, his idea of overlapping consensus and his discussion of the importance of practical reason. Indeed, in the midst of his argument for reasonable pluralism, he makes a claim that is reminiscent of James.

> If sound, these remarks suggest that *in philosophy questions at the most fundamental level are not usually settled by conclusive argument* [emphasis added]. What is obvious to some persons and accepted as a basic idea is unintelligible to others. The way to resolve this matter is to consider after due reflection which view, when fully worked out, offers the most coherent and convincing account. About this, of course, judgements may differ.[26]

In this statement of the grounds for pluralism, Rawls argues from a sceptical position regarding final theories about the world: 'philosophical questions ... are not settled by conclusive argument'. This does not mean, however, that Rawls is a relativist (as perhaps Walzer would be eager to conclude) or a sceptic. Rather, Rawls leaves open the possibility that there are some criteria for deciding among views of the world, namely, that a good account must be 'coherent and convincing'. Nonetheless, Rawls leaves it up to us to pragmatically work out the parameters of coherence among our diverse comprehensive schemes. As far as the principles of social cooperation go, Rawls states in the next paragraph that the 'reasonable is public'. We work the criteria out publicly according to what works best to ensure cooperation in light of the fact of diversity. Thus Rawls' pragmatism is located in his emphasis on the *political* nature of liberalism: toleration is a pragmatic *political* value.

Rawls has further clarified this in his 'Reply to Habermas' where he insists that political liberalism is political and 'leaves philosophy as it is'.[27] What he means by this is that the ideas of political liberalism are worked out among us as we pragmatically define what we are willing to accept, or, put more pragmatically, as we define what works for us. He further states that his theory is simply a reasonable 'conjecture' and that it may be revisable given further experience and reflection.[28] Finally, Rawls explicitly denies that political liberalism offers a theory of truth. He says: 'The use of the concept of truth is not rejected or questioned, but left to comprehensive doctrines to use or deny, or use some other idea instead.'[29] Thus Rawls suggests that we can sidestep the issue of truth by turning to the political ideas of reasonableness, overlapping consensus and tolerance: 'The reasonable does, or course, express a reflective attitude to toleration, since it recognizes the burdens of judgement, and this in turn leads to liberty of conscience and freedom of thought.'[30] Political liberalism seeks pragmatically to facilitate consensus building among comprehensive doctrines by tolerating liberty without advocating that liberty is a substantive good. Rawls' discussion, like Walzer's, thus fits nicely into the tradition of pragmatic thought about toleration.

However, Rawls, tries to avoid the slippery slope of Rorty's liberal ironism. Rorty claims that there could be public or shared consensus despite the fact of a private 'ironic' attitude. Unfortunately, it seems that there is no way to build up the bases for the development of public consensus if individual judgement is not constrained – as in Rawls – by an ideal of practical reason. Rorty claims, in a passage that sounds like Rawls, that: 'For public purposes, it does not matter if everybody's final vocabulary is different, as long as there is enough overlap so that everybody has some words with which to express the desirability of entering into other people's fantasies as well as into one's own.'[31] Rorty's idea of overlap is not, however, the same as Rawls' idea of 'overlapping consensus'. The crucial difference is that Rawls supposes both that individuals are committed to some comprehensive doctrine and that they can come to publicly agree about the conditions for cooperation in shared social space. Rorty, on the other hand, does not require that individuals have any commitment to a comprehensive doctrine. Rawls' idea of the reasonable allows for greater possibilities for agreement than does Rorty's private ironism.[32] Rawls makes a strong claim about the kind of public reasonableness that is necessary for democratic politics to function: individuals in the public sphere must be committed to the 'burdens of judgement'. Rawls' project can develop further than Rorty's because it demands some shared commitment to an idea of the reasonable even amid diversity. This is what he defines as 'reasonable pluralism'.

The pragmatic pluralism of John Lachs

A pragmatic idea of pluralism has been fleshed out recently by John Lachs. In his account of the plurality of what he calls 'human natures', Lachs ties pluralism explicitly to toleration. Lachs discusses three types of facts: objective, conventional and choice-inclusive. Objective facts are those things in the world that we discover as the result of inquiry: they are the given stuff of experience, such as the fact that ice is slick. Conventional facts are those things that depend entirely upon us: they are entirely the result of our choices, such as the fact that we call ice 'ice'. Finally, choice-inclusive facts are those facts that are based upon certain given aspects of the world while also relying upon our choices, such as the fact that we play ice hockey in the Winter Olympics. This last fact is based upon certain objective features of the world (pucks and skates slide over ice) but is also based upon certain conventional choices (we could after all, with modern technology, play hockey in summer).

Just as William James tried to avoid the extremes of metaphysical realism and/or anti-realism, Lachs wants to deny that our world is made up entirely of either objective or conventional facts. James states: 'The world is in so far forth a pluralism of which the unity is not fully experienced as yet'; and experience grows from within, 'by its edges'.[33] Moreover, 'there may ultimately never be an all-form at all, that the substance of reality may never get totally collected, that some of it may remain outside of the largest combination of it ever made, and that a distributive form of reality, the each-form, is logically as acceptable and empirically as probable as the all-form'.[34] Thus, there is no possibility of reaching a final synthesis of the whole. What remains is, at best, a plurality on its way towards final unity. If this is the case, given that certain blindness which afflicts us, we ought to remain tolerant.

The difficulty we face is a certain lack of modesty. The objectivist view forgets that many of our categories are 'constructed' according to our purposes. The conventionalist view forgets that there is a world out-there to which we must respond. Lachs concludes: 'A sensible philosophy must, then, acknowledge the existence of both objective and conventional facts.'[35] Moreover, we must also admit that the intersection of these two types of facts in 'choice-inclusive facts' constitutes the important ethical and political portion of our experience. Concepts that Lachs views as choice-inclusive include 'human', 'person', 'healthy', 'living', 'intelligent' and others. These are crucial ethical and political concepts that establish criteria by which we distribute goods to one another: a 'person' for example is an object of respect and a bearer of rights. The definition of these terms 'requires a decision about how to weigh each, and that, in turn, mobilizes the values and purposes of the community. The coldly cognitive quickly leads to the normative for its supplementation.'[36]

As an example consider the concept of 'person'. Who or what should be called a person? Should a foetus, for example, be called a person? Such a question cannot be answered merely by appealing to objective facts about foetuses; it requires a value judgement about whether we are willing to grant the foetus status as a moral patient and political recognition as a bearer of rights. For Lachs the concept of 'person' is a choice-inclusive category. In Walzer's language the concept of 'person' depends upon our 'social-meanings', meanings which are relative to history and culture: 'All distributions are just or unjust relative to the social meanings of the goods at stake.'[37] For Rawls, such a concept may be defined either in political terms – who is a citizen – or in terms of the moral or metaphysical world-view of a comprehensive doctrine. Rawls defines persons politically as those who are 'capable of being normal and fully cooperating members of society over a complete life'.[38] This is undoubtedly one of Lachs' choice-inclusive definitions: it is based upon facts (we can cooperate) and values (we should cooperate). Moreover, it clearly is an important part of the way we distribute goods among ourselves.

Like Lachs and Walzer, Rawls admits a plurality of possible definitions of human being: 'There are many aspects of our nature that can be singled out as particularly significant depending on our aim and point of view.'[39] Rawls' goal, however, is to discover some political consensus despite the plurality of meanings found within differing comprehensive doctrines. This is a pragmatic move which tries to avoid the slide into relativism. Our political agreement about a set of meanings that is compatible with the plurality of comprehensive doctrines is purely pragmatic: we want to be able to coexist with others despite our disagreement at the level of morality and metaphysics.

As noted above, 'pluralism', as described by Walzer or Rorty, threatens to devolve at this point into a pernicious form of relativism if we divorce our criteria entirely from facts about the world. Rorty, for example, seems to argue that there is no objective definition of personhood. He even claims that the idea of 'human solidarity' may be a contingent, albeit powerful, 'piece of rhetoric'.[40] Rorty wants to emphasize the fact that human solidarity is an idea whose meaning we are still in the process of working out. One must be careful, however, not to conclude that it is a meaningless idea simply because we work it out for ourselves. Rather, the pragmatic approach is to admit plurality with the hope that the vast majority of us, even despite our disagreements, will come to share this choice-inclusive idea as we work together to clarify our values and beliefs. Walzer seems to recognize this in his consideration of 'postmodern toleration' and the 'divided selves' of postmodernity. Walzer admits that we must be careful not to go too far in the relativist direction he himself hints at: 'Radical freedom is thin stuff unless it exists within a world that offers it significant resistance.'[41] Rather, Walzer recognizes that there are some facts about the world that simply cannot be erased by the postmodern celebration of difference. Walzer states that we belong to groups, despite our radical freedom. He also claims that these group affiliations and the desire of these groups for recognition form the locus for tolerant politics. These are facts in the world that cannot be denied.

We are left, then, with a dialectical view of human nature. Individuals share certain features in common as a result of our membership in the human species. But we also differ in important and interesting ways. We might argue, as Martha Nussbaum has, that there are many features of human nature that are shared despite our differences.[42] We are human animals who suffer, love and think. Pragmatic toleration wants to recognize this commonality at the level of basic human being without telling us how to suffer, who to love, or what to think. Lachs concludes: 'Our shared nature forms the foundation of decency, our divergent natures provide the ground of toleration.'[43] Toleration results from a recognition of our shared need to form a community despite the fact of our individual differences.

Conclusion

We use the ideas of 'person', 'human', etc. to define choice-inclusive norms. A person is one who should be respected, even though it is still an open question of who or what counts as a person. This would seem to mark the limits of toleration: we tolerate those who share our basic choice-inclusive norms, even if they apply these differently. We do not tolerate those who do not share these norms at all. We do not tolerate those who do not respect persons or who do not tolerate others. Such people would be unreasonable, in Rawls' sense, for they fail to meet the intersubjective standard for participation in political society. Rather than tolerate such individuals, we educate them so that they may come to share the basic choice-inclusive norms, the basic pragmatic sense of reasonableness, in which toleration can be expressed. Thus toleration is one of the most important of our choice-inclusive norms: it joins the fact of diversity with the value of peaceful coexistence in political society. It is a pragmatic value because it is our attempt to work out, among ourselves, the basic practical conditions for social cooperation.

This is not to say that toleration is groundless or relative in a pernicious sense. Indeed, toleration has its limits, imposed on the one side by nature and on the other by our shared social values. Lachs' account of pluralism, for example, admits some variability with regard to our social values but recognizes that some things are simply facts of the matter that cannot be disputed. Just as the tolerant can condemn the intolerant for their intolerance, a pluralist can say that some things are simply false. Pluralism does not deny that there are standards or criteria of judgement. These standards come from two directions. On the one hand, the world of objective facts provides us with an immutable set of standards; on the other hand, our ethical and political values supply us with another set, more mutable perhaps, but also limited by context and consistency. Pluralism acknowledges the intersection of these sets of standards. Is a foetus a 'person'? The answer depends in part upon the way the world is (foetuses are organic objects dependent upon their mothers for sustenance); it also depends upon our values (do we want to provide foetuses with rights? Is this consistent with other applications of the concept of person?). Relativism denies all standards implying that we could call clock radios 'persons' and give them rights if we so desired ('after all, it is all relative ...'). Such a view is reckless and absurd. From Rawls' point of view, it would be unreasonable. Lachs' brand of pluralism, in opposition to standardless relativism, wants to recognize some plasticity in our values while denying that values are entirely groundless. Lachs' pluralism can thus help to flesh out the details of Rawls' account of the reasonable.

Moreover, and here is where Rawls offers an important contribution to pragmatism, the pluralist can remain committed to an idea of developing an overlapping consensus without succumbing to Rorty's private irony. It is pragmatically true that liberal democratic politics is the best defence of diversity. To put it more bluntly, toleration works (in the pragmatic cash-value sense) to fulfil the diverse goals of the individuals who constitute diverse societies like our own. Pragmatic toleration recognizes the facts of the world as including both diversity and the general human desire for peaceful coexistence. Toleration of the kind espoused by Lachs and Rawls is the best way pragmatically to deal with these facts.

Tolerant politics is based upon the idea that we ought to agree to allow ourselves to disagree about the direction of our shared life together and about the value of our private decisions. This normative claim is grounded, not in some metaphysical truth about the nature of human being but, rather, in the pragmatic fact that we are better able to go on with our diverse projects if we are tolerant towards one another. Liberal toleration is thus pragmatically grounded in the desire for peaceful co-existence that leads us to recognize the objective fact of our diversity and our need for cooperation. There are many ways that we might choose to determine ourselves both publicly and privately; however, this diversity of possible lives is constrained by a general definition of the good (embodied in what we call our basic rights). This choice-inclusive standard includes respect for autonomy and toleration: it states that we think it is good for us to recognize our differences.

Rawls, Walzer, Rorty and Lachs agree to this commitment to toleration. Lachs expresses this in an ontological vein when he argues that we must admit that there is a plurality of human natures. He concludes that a recognition of such plurality results in toleration: 'we will understand people better, and even if we give them wide berth, we will be more disposed to tolerate them'.[44] This sounds like a noble liberal ideal, however, it is not unproblematic. Lachs' book ends on a pessimistic note: 'my conclusions will have no validity at all save for those whose nature – being similar to mine – prescribes for them a similar way of life'.[45] This seems to echo Rorty's ironic conclusions about liberalism. The reason for this pessimism and irony is that, according to Lachs' pluralism, there may be no common element that all human beings share. Thus in a pluralistic universe, tolerance may mean agreeing among ourselves to be tolerant while recognizing that we may inhabit different moral worlds and that we may have to resort to 'Hobbesian reminders' (as Williams noted) as we defend tolerance against intolerance.

Such a conclusion poses an ongoing problem for our political community. When must we fight those whose difference consists in repugnant, anti-social, unjust or intolerant behaviour? Lachs' tolerant pluralism asks us simply to avoid these others as best we can. Unfortunately the fact of diversity also means that

occasionally we must fight, although such a fight should be pragmatically directed towards the goal of peaceful coexistence. Rawls
reaches a similarly cautious conclusion with regard to his overlapping consensus. Social stability requires overlapping consensus;
however, Rawls notes that there remains the possibility that intolerant or unreasonable individuals and groups may disrupt this consensus. He hopes that such groups 'may not be strong enough to
undermine the substantive justice of the regime. This is the hope;
there can be no guarantee.'[46] Thus Rawls, like Lachs and James,
admits that political stability is fragile – an object of hope – and
that it is up to us, pragmatically, to work out for ourselves the
political conditions that make consensus and stability possible.

Notes

1. Karl-Otto Apel, 'Plurality of the Good?', *Ratio Juris*, 10:2, June 1997,
   p. 201.
2. Bernard Williams, 'Toleration: an Impossible Virtue' in David Heyd
   (ed.) *Toleration: An Elusive Virtue*, Princeton, NJ: Princeton University
   Press, 1996, p. 26.
3. See Barbara Herman, 'Pluralism and the Community of Moral Judgment' in David Heyd (ed.) *Toleration: An Elusive Virtue*.
4. William James, 'On a Certain Blindness in Human Beings' in *Talks to
   Teachers on Psychology and to Students on Some of Life's Ideals*, Cambridge,
   MA: Harvard University Press, 1983, p. 149. Also see my discussion of
   James in Chapter 5.
5. Cf. Rorty, *Contingency, Irony, Solidarity*, Cambridge: Cambridge University Press, 1989, p. 38.
6. John Dewey, *Reconstruction in Philosophy*, Boston: The Beacon Press, 1957,
   chapter 2, pp. 45–6.
7. For example in 'Individualism Old and New' in John Dewey, *The Later
   Works*, vol. 5, Carbondale, IL: Southern Illinois University Press, 1984.
8. 'Liberalism and Social Action', chapter 2 in John Dewey, *The Later
   Works*, vol. 11, Carbondale, IL: Southern Illinois University Press, 1987.
9. John Dewey, *The Public and its Problems*, New York: Henry Holt and Co.,
   1927, 1954, p. 51.

10. John Dewey, 'Individualism Old and New' in *The Later Works*, p. 27.

11. For a discussion of the American emphasis on the individual see John Lachs, *A Community of Individuals*, New York: Routledge, 2003, chapter 15.

12. For a discussion of the difference between tolerance and relativism cf. John W. Cook, *Morality and Cultural Differences*, Oxford: Oxford University Press, 1999, especially pp. 26–9 where he discusses political liberalism.

13. John Rawls, *A Theory of Justice*, Cambridge, MA: Harvard University Press, 1971, pp. 94, 29. Michael Sandel criticizes this as the 'priority of plurality over unity' (Sandel, *Liberalism and the Limits of Justice*, Cambridge: Cambridge University Press, 1982, pp. 50–3). A useful introduction to this debate is Will Kymlicka, 'Liberal Individualism and Liberal Neutrality', *Ethics*, 99 (July 1989) reprinted in James P. Sterba, *Justice: Alternative Political Perspectives*, 2nd edition, Belmont, CA: Wadsworth, 1992.

14. John Rawls, *Justice as Fairness: A Restatement*, Cambridge, MA: Harvard University Press, 2001, p. 3.

15. John Rawls, *Political Liberalism*, New York: Columbia University Press, 1995, p. 44.

16. Critics of liberalism such as Catherine MacKinnon have denied that the state could be a 'neutral' or 'impartial' distributor of goods (Mackinnon, *Toward a Feminist Theory of the State*, Cambridge, MA: Harvard University Press, 1991). This critical perspective was perhaps most forcefully articulated in the context of toleration by Herbert Marcuse in 'Repressive Tolerance' in Wolff, Moore and Marcuse (eds) *A Critique of Pure Tolerance*, Boston: Beacon Press, 1969.

17. Cf, Rawls, *Justice as Fairness*, p. 36.

18. For further discussion of the political nature of Rawls' toleration see Kok-Chor Tan, 'Liberalism in Rawls' Law of Peoples', *Ethics*, 108, January 1998, especially footnote 18. Also for a discussion of Rawls and truth see David Estlund, 'The Insularity of the Reasonable: Why Political Liberalism Must Admit the Truth', *Ethics*, 108, January 1998. Estlund concludes that Rawls must admit 'a single point of contact with the moral truth that permits political liberalism to float freely at all other points' (p. 254). I am sympathetic to this reading of Rawls provided that the idea of 'moral truth' is pragmatically defined.

19. Michael Walzer, *Spheres of Justice*, New York: Basic Books, 1983, p. 6.

20. *Ibid.*, p. 312.

21. Walzer, *On Toleration*, New Haven, CT: Yale University Press, 1997, p. 5.
22. *Ibid.*, p. 5.
23. For a critical discussion of Walzer's *On Toleration* see Hans Oberdieck, *Tolerance: Between Forbearance and Acceptance*, Lanham, MD: Rowman and Littlefield, 2001.
24. This discussion is based upon Rawls, *Political Liberalism*, pp. 54–8.
25. Aristotle, *Nicomachean Ethics*, trans. Terence Irwin, Indianapolis: Hackett Publishing, 1985, p. 1106.
26. Rawls, *Political Liberalism*, p. 53.
27. Rawls, 'Reply to Habermas', *Journal of Philosophy*, 92:3, 1995, p. 134.
28. *Ibid.*, p. 139.
29. *Ibid.*, p. 150.
30. *Ibid.*
31. Rorty, 'Private Irony and Liberal Hope' in *Contingency, Irony, and Solidarity*, Cambridge: Cambridge University Press, pp. 92–3. Rorty discusses Rawls and understands him as a pragmatist on pp. 57–8.
32. For a discussion of the limits of private ironism, see Gary Gutting, *Pragmatic Liberalism and the Critique of Modernity*, Cambridge: Cambridge University Press, 1999, pp. 58–67.
33. William James, 'A World of Pure Experience' in *Essays in Radical Empiricism*, Cambridge: Harvard University Press, 1976, pp. 43, 42.
34. James, *A Pluralistic Universe*, Cambridge, MA: Harvard University Press, 1977, p. 20.
35. Lachs, *The Relevance of Philosophy to Life*, Nashville: Vanderbilt University Press, p. 246.
36. *Ibid.*, p. 248.
37. Walzer, *Spheres of Justice*, p. 9.
38. Rawls, *Political Liberalism*, p. 301.
39. *Ibid.*, pp. 299–300.
40. Rorty, *Contingency, Irony, and Solidarity*, p. 192.
41. Walzer, *On Toleration*, p. 92.
42. Martha C. Nussbaum, 'In Defense of Universal Values' in *Women and Human Development*, Cambridge: Cambridge University Press, 2000.
43. Lachs, *A Community of Individuals*, p. 55.
44. Lachs, *The Relevance of Philosophy to Life*, p. 253.
45. *Ibid.*, p. 266.
46. Rawls, *Political Liberalism*, p. 65.

9

Conclusion: Socrates Beyond Liberalism

The pragmatic ideal of contemporary political liberalism has its limits. Rawls, for example, is focused on generating a political account that does not say anything about more substantive views of the good life. Such a political approach is useful in its place: it helps us negotiate liveable institutions in a world of diversity. But if we want to know how to lead a good life – not merely how to get along with others in a world of diversity – then we will want a more substantive approach to the question of ethics. A more substantive account of tolerance aims beyond mere overlapping consensus about tolerance. It grounds tolerance in a substantive ideal of human flourishing. And it tells us why tolerance is good, not merely that people grudgingly agree to be tolerant. Pragmatic consensus appears to be inadequate to answer the question of why tolerance is good. But this claim appears to beg the question of knowledge. What is knowledge, if not consensus? With this question we return to Socrates and the link between tolerance and the philosophical life.

As mentioned in Chapter 1, Socrates argues in the *Charmides* that temperance (*sophrosyne*) and the task of self-examination are closely intertwined. But self-examination is also intertwined with the dialogical process. Philosophy asks us to critically examine ourselves; but we do this by examining each other. This process begins by reflecting upon our assumptions. There is simply no thinking without assumptions. But there is no good thinking without this form of self-conscious self-criticism. And yes, this is an assumption – but one that is justified through this very process. We do learn the standards of good thinking from others. And we develop our ideas through dialogue with others. But the social element of dialogue does not mean that truth itself is a result of pragmatic consensus. Knowledge does result from social inter-action. But this does not mean that the object of knowledge is somehow entirely produced by social interaction. In general, dia-logue helps us to discover truths – not to invent them. But, with regard to social and political 'truths', i.e., those 'choice-inclusive' truths of social life, there is an interesting interplay between dis-covery and invention. Some truths are contingently located in the choices of people. Consider the claim that 'toleration is good in pluralistic societies'. Rawls would justify this claim by appealing to consensus: different members of the diverse society will agree with him about this claim, albeit for different reasons. But the overlapping consensus itself helps to make the claim true: flourish-ing pluralistic societies are those that are able to achieve overlap-ping consensus about this claim.

My point here is that even though it is primarily knowledge (and not truth) that is developed in dialogue with others, there are some truths that are both found in and created by dialogue. More concretely, we find in certain sorts of dialogue that tol-erance is a precondition of these sorts of dialogue. We learn that tolerance is good only when we are already engaged in genuine dialogue. In other words, we discover together that tolerance is a necessary feature of the process of communal discovery.

Genuine dialogues are supposed to produce truth. Plato says, in the *Republic*, for example, that dialectic is the ability 'to give an account of the being of each thing' while also being able to 'survive all refutation, as if in a battle, striving to judge things not in accordance with opinion but in accordance with being'.[1] But it is the dialogical process that allows us to know whether we behold the truth or not. Even Kant held that truth is revealed through the dialogical process of critical reasoning, calling the consensus developed in community with others the *touchstone of truth*: 'The touchstone whereby we decide whether our holding a thing to be true is conviction or mere persuasion is therefore external, namely, the possibility of communicating it and of finding it to be valid for all human reason.'[2] Ideally, we work together to discover those opinions that are best justified by way of dialogical interaction.

Since tolerance is the virtue that makes this communal pursuit of wisdom possible, it is difficult to engage in a dialogical investigation of tolerance without begging the question. A dialogue about tolerance can thus be accused of being, in some sense, circular. But this circle may also indicate the unavoidable fact that tolerance is good. At least it is necessary for the dialogical process; and if we think that the dialogical process is good, then tolerance will be good. It might be possible that there are those who reject both dialogue and tolerance. But such intolerant beings would be difficult to communicate with. Indeed, it is even difficult to imagine that those who advocate such an extreme form of intolerance could participate in the pragmatic project of building consensus. Thus it is possible that underlying the seemingly merely pragmatic consensus of political liberalism is a deeper commitment to tolerance at the level of commitment to dialogical interaction. In conclusion, I will respond explicitly to one critique of liberalism in order to make a final point about the difference between political toleration and the individual virtue of tolerance.

The problem of politics

Tolerant government ought to allow citizens to pursue their own good in their own way within reasonable limits. John Stuart Mill's 'liberty principle' serves as one well-known standard here. For Mill, harm is the limit of liberty. This makes for a nice theory, which accords quite well with common sense. The government should leave individuals alone, unless they are hurting others. In practice, however, it is quite difficult to determine whether or not harm has been done because in a pluralistic society there will be different definitions of harm. It may, in fact, be impossible to stipulate a neutral theory of privacy or harm, just as it is impossible for a state to be entirely neutral. As Iris Young has argued, following upon insights derived from Marx and from critical theorists: 'The idea of the neutral state that stands above the particular interests and conflicts of civil society is a myth.'[3] Striking a similar note, Alasdair MacIntyre writes: 'the modern state is never a neutral arbiter of conflicts, but is always to some degree itself a party to social conflict' because 'it acts in the interests of particular and highly contestable conceptions of liberty and property'.[4] To make this point more clearly, we might consider the idea of private property (where the adjective 'private' is supposed to indicate that property owners are entitled to do whatever they want with such property, provided they do not cause a public nuisance). Those who believe that private property is a natural right will view certain actions (from theft to taxation) as harmful, while those who do not accept the notion of private property may not view these same actions as harmful. In the last couple of centuries, wars were fought about whether private property was in fact social property. Those who advocate redistributions of property (whether the Marxist idea of 'expropriating the expropriators' or the Rawlsian idea of the difference principle) will wonder whether a state grounded on the notion of private property begs certain important questions. Moreover, those who do not accept the idea of private property may see the supposed 'private' actions of property owners as causing substantial harms (to labourers or to the environment) that ought to be regulated. At the same time, such 'harms' are either tolerated by societies that view private property as so sacrosanct that it cannot be violated or these results are simply not viewed as genuine harms.

A more substantive form of liberalism would clearly define both harm and privacy and admit that these definitions, while attempting to be objective and true, are not neutral. But if the most widely acceptable form of liberalism is merely pragmatic or political in Rawls' sense, then this substantive liberalism cannot be politically effective.

One might ask whether the idea of state neutrality and notions such as 'harm' and 'privacy' are merely ideological disguises for substantive claims about what is good. For example, when the state allows pornography, is this an implicit claim about the fact that pornography is good? Catherine MacKinnon has argued, following Marxist ideas about ideology, that toleration of pornography is actually a form of male-dominance hiding under the ideology of free speech: 'Liberalism has never understood this reality of pornography: the free so-called speech of men silences the free speech of women.'[5] From MacKinnon's perspective, the free speech defence of pornography begs the question in favour of men about what is private, what is mere speech and what is harmful. The same sort of argument could be applied to a variety of issues. What about when the state allows (or doesn't allow) abortions? How about when the state allows (or doesn't allow) children to pray in school? Or when the state allows (or doesn't allow) homosexuals to marry? What about when the state uses tax money, student fees or structures the tax system so as to support organizations such as churches, museums, youth organizations, etc.? And along the same lines, what about when the state gives tax breaks to corporations, home-owners and parents? The problem is that it is nearly impossible for state decisions not to violate official state neutrality and sanction certain activities as good, while condemning other actions as unworthy of support or toleration.

A more substantive political ideology would bite the bullet and argue that certain actions – pornography, homosexuality, etc. – are good or not. And it would also provide clear criteria, based upon metaphysical foundations, that would allow us to define exactly what sorts of activities are supposed to be private and thus to be tolerated or are supposed to be harmful and thus not to be tolerated. But this runs counter to the notion of reasonable pluralism found in the Rawlsian view, wherein such criteria and the metaphysics upon which they are grounded are contestable at the level of comprehensive schemes. The pragmatic consensus about political principles of toleration leaves the substantive questions unanswered.

When the state seeks to mitigate 'harm', it can never really be neutral. For example, when the state outlaws drug use or when it mandates age requirements for the consumption of nicotine and alcohol, such actions can be seen as a form of paternalism, which says that people should not be allowed to pursue things they want. The same goes for issues such as the following: seatbelt laws for motorists and helmet laws for motorcyclists; the requirement that children be educated; prohibitions on suicide and euthanasia; laws against prostitution or certain forms of sexuality; etc. The problem is that states routinely make concrete decisions about harms, which from certain perspectives will inevitably seem to be patronizing and illiberal.

In order to avoid the complaint that these interventions are unjustified, we need substantive claims about what is good or true. From a point of view that holds toleration up as a primary good, the only justification for intervention is to protect privacy and to minimize harm. The difficulty here is not one of developing political consensus but, rather, an epistemological problem of knowing what is harmful and what is private. Without a metaphysics and epistemology that allows us to resolve these questions, these issues will remain muddled and subject to complaints about ethnocentrism, cultural imperialism or other forms of bias. In other words, the definition of neutrality ought to be a factual question based upon certain truths about human beings and not a matter of pragmatic consensus. If it is merely consensual, it becomes difficult to define harm or 'privacy' in any meaningful way, because, after all, the consensus may shift as the population does. But if we espouse a more substantial ideology, we will find it hard to achieve consensus amid the fact of diversity.

One solution might be to admit the plausibility of pluralism. Pluralism is the idea that there may be more than one mode of life that is good; but it is not a disavowal of all standards. The state should not restrict its citizens' ethical choices because it is possible that many of these diverse choices are good. One can admit value pluralism without falling into a pernicious form of relativism, as argued in Chapter 2. At least, the pluralistic claim is not itself relative: it is meant to articulate a truth about human life. Moreover, there is no contradiction in saying that different things are each good in their own way. Pluralism is opposed to a perfectionist view of politics that wants the state to promote one exclusive view of the good. This idea of perfectionist politics cannot account for the diverse views of the good, which are possessed by different individuals. Perfectionist politics is thus one-sided, dogmatic, intolerant and tyrannical. A tolerant approach attempts to avoid this problem by restraining state power and by allowing individuals to develop their own private morality within the plurality of possible views of the good. Such a view emphasizes liberty over conformity and recognizes that political authority tends to be opposed to individual liberty. It recognizes that it is good for human beings to decide for themselves about what is good and that state intervention undermines this process of autonomous commitment. Within a point of view that recognizes that there is a plurality of the good and that autonomous commitment is essential for individual morality, toleration will be viewed as an ideal goal.

The difficulty is to reconcile the ideal of toleration with the fact that, as an ideal, toleration is not itself neutral and that pluralism is a non-relative account of the good. A Rawlsian approach holds out hope for attaining pragmatic consensus among those who do not share the commitments of substantive liberalism, as well as among those who deny the truth of pluralism. But the worry is that the consensus achieved in this way will be too vague to be of use; or indeed, that there will be no consensus, as is the case in the

United States, with regard to issues such as abortion or homo-sexuality. And a further worry is that if this consensus is merely a *modus vivendi*, then as soon as the power differentials shift, the consensus will fail.

I fear that at the level of politics there is no adequate solution to these problems. We want more here than we will be able to obtain. We would like to have consensus about harm and the proper limits of state power. But in a tolerant, pluralistic society there will be no such consensus. Nonetheless, toleration remains an important principle as we work towards consensus, in part because it is some-thing like a condition for the possibility of developing genuine con-sensus. But again the problem is reiterated if we consider that there will be those who reject even the idea that consensus is of value.

Pluralistic convergence and fanaticism

There are no easy answers to the problem of political toleration. In this sense, the question of individual tolerance is easier to answer. Indeed, the previous chapters have attempted to show that there is a wide range of agreement about the fact that toler-ance is good for individuals. While there are lingering questions, hopefully, this book has shown that the Western tradition is com-mitted to tolerance and that tolerance can be seen as good from a variety of perspectives. In other words, there is a pluralistic con-vergence towards tolerance: many different good approaches to the ethical life converge and mutually support the idea of toler-ance. The best activities are those that are supported by many dif-ferent value schemes. We can be reasonably certain that we are making wise decisions and good choices when these choices and decisions are supported by a plurality of different arguments. This pluralistic convergence does not only apply at the level of ethical theories, but it is also hoped that there can be convergence of diverse views of the good life at the level of religion and culture.

The idea of pluralistic convergence is similar to Rawls' idea of overlapping consensus. But one of the difficulties of Rawls' approach is that he claims that those who dogmatically hold on to intolerant comprehensive doctrines must loosen their beliefs enough to tolerate others.[6] His point is a psychological one about the general weakness of commitment and a historical one about the continued decline of belief in comprehensive doctrines. Both of these are necessary for the eventual triumph of liberal toleration in Rawls' sense. But Rawls may be expressing a form of utopian hope here: recent history shows us that fanatics can still wreak havoc on tolerant societies. My own hope for pluralistic convergence also demands a diminution in the fanatical zealotry with which believers pursue their comprehensive doctrines. The existential and pragmatic approaches to religion, described in previous chapters, hold that it is possible for the believer to hold on to her account of the good without thereby rejecting the other's idea of the good. Inward sincerity of belief is not necessarily tied to fanaticism: one can be tolerant and sincere in one's own beliefs, so long as one restrains oneself with regard to acting to negate the beliefs or activities of others. Fanaticism is a matter of the vehemence and single-mindedness of sincere belief. Fanatics suffer from immoderate pride as they intolerantly force their beliefs upon others in a world of diversity. Sincere believers who keep to themselves are not a threat to others and can certainly be tolerated. But the sort of fanaticism that cannot be tolerated is the sort that utilizes violence to disseminate its truth. As should be clear by now, this sort of fanaticism runs counter to the very idea of philosophical enlightenment described throughout. Indeed, it runs counter to the idea that there could be something like a pluralistic convergence obtained through reasoned dialogue and not by force. A tolerant pluralist must admit that there might be more than one well-justified comprehensive theory of the good life. But admitting this does not mean that one cannot remain inwardly sincere in one's commitment to one's own best theory. Indeed, a commitment to Socratic methodology requires us to keep our best theories open for continued criticism.

Tolerance means only that one cannot utilize violence and force to disseminate one's theory. Those fanatics who do employ violence are, by definition, intolerant. And the tolerant are entitled to employ violence in defence of tolerance, according to ideas of justified violence. This may seem to be a version of the 'paradox of toleration' discussed in previous chapters; and it may push us towards the same sorts of problems indicated in the previous section. At least, this claim risks begging the question about who, in fact, is tolerant or not, by opening up the door towards tolerant uses of violence. The difference in character between tolerant uses of violence and the violence of fanatics is seen in a willingness to recognize limits to the use of violence. What might be called 'tolerant violence' will be committed to modest goals and will be primarily concerned with peace.[7] Fanatical violence is aimed at total conversion or total extermination of the other. Tolerant violence is aimed only at resisting fanaticism and establishing coexistence with the hope of producing a sort of pluralistic convergence. This means that violence employed by the tolerant will be restrained by these modest goals. The just war theory thus provides a set of constraints on violence that embody the spirit of tolerance. The goal of a just war, according to Walzer's influential paradigm, is not to convert or exterminate an enemy.[8] Rather, it is to defend the system of nations and national sovereignty and, possibly, to defend the human rights of people suffering under intolerant regimes. But this means that violence used in the name of toleration and guided by the virtue of tolerance will be appropriately restrained.

I am not very hopeful about the possibility for the formation of a real consensus about any other than the most basic principles of justice. The best we can do is open the space in which plural voices can be heard and criticized. This idea does call for a set of procedural norms based upon the idea of toleration. These norms will include basic human rights. My own modest conclusion is, however, that the norms established by the idea of critical moral toleration are quite limited in scope. All that the norm of toleration asks is that we openly criticize theories and arguments and that we refrain from violence. Certain political principles follow from this including freedom of speech, assembly, etc. However, it is unlikely that something like Rawls' second principle of justice (the difference principle) can be supported in this way.

The idea of pluralistic convergence provides the hope that facilitates the ideal of toleration. That is, a proper understanding of pluralism leads us to the conclusion that convergence towards consensus is possible. It is this possibility which in turn stimulates our conversations, dialogues and critiques and which forms the basis of the philosophical community. To be a Socrates, in the face of tragic disagreement, one must remain hopeful. Indeed in the *Apology*, Socrates tells us that to give up hope in the face of death is to fall back into a form of unjustified dogmatic certainty about the future. The point is that we simply do not know whether there will be a pluralistic convergence; from this sceptical self-restraint comes hope – a thin hope, but hope nonetheless. The idea of pluralistic convergence does not eliminate the fact that within the plurality of good arguments there will be divergence and disagreement. However, this divergence ought not to lead to fragmentation, apathy and relativism. Recall that pluralism is the idea that there are multiple possibilities for good, that different arguments can be valid and that there is no priority or hierarchy of goods that can finally resolve all value conflicts. Nonetheless, pluralism holds that divergent possibilities can still be called 'good' or 'valid' without contradiction. It also holds that value conflicts provide opportunities for synthesis, not walls to communication. The hope of pluralistic convergence motivates the use of the imagination, the critical faculties of dialogue, and our communal interest in mutual understanding.

Conclusion: beyond the cave

To develop the conditions for the possibility of pluralistic convergence, we must work to make our institutions and our lives more
tolerant. This has been a problem since Socrates. The intolerant
cave dwellers of Plato's *Republic* had been perverted, such that
they were willing to kill the philosopher who wanted to free them.
Thinking beings would, we would think, at least listen to the
philosopher who claims to bring them news of the world beyond
the cave. We would think that thinking beings would naturally
turn around to search for the source of light, naturally question
their own assumptions. But the dogmatism and intolerance of
closed cultures and bad education enslave us and prevent us from
questioning our assumptions. Indeed, intolerance can pervert us
such that we do not want to be bothered with the new and different
to such an extent that we are willing to kill the other who disturbs
our equanimity.

Philosophers should help individuals resist intolerance by
reminding us about what we do not know, so that we keep that
habit of open-mindedness that allows us to continue questioning
in pursuit of truth. The two most famous Socratic aphorisms –
'The unexamined life is not worth living' and 'The only thing I
know is that I know nothing' – form the recipe for the ideal of
critical moral toleration I have defended in this book. And the
communities of inquiry created in the Socratic dialogues form the
model for the idea of the philosophical community I have
described in these pages. Socrates' ideal of the ethical life is one
spent critically examining himself in community with others.
Members of this critical dialogical community must be tolerant.
The Socratic inquirer does not make claims to wisdom that result
in active negation of the other members of the philosophical community. Rather, he listens attentively to his interlocutors, hoping
to learn from them. And when he suspects that he knows the

truth, he pushes them towards it with words only and not with deeds. The distinction between word and deed is essential here. When I tolerate something I refrain from actively negating it in deed. But this does not mean I need to refrain from criticizing it with words. Thus tolerance can and should be linked to critical questioning. Indeed, members of the philosophical community commit themselves to being questioned critically in this way, trusting that the other members of the community who question them will tolerate their mistakes, while also helping to correct them without using anything other than the force of reason.

It should be obvious then, that the philosophical community is a community of speech, based upon a commitment to truth and respect for the power of reason. While it may be a model for more concrete sorts of political communities, it is limited as a model insofar as it does not have resources with which to deal with evil or obnoxious persons who are not respectful of tolerant speech. Political communities are communities of deeds as well as speech: political communities have the power of life and death over their members. But philosophers renounce their capacity for deeds insofar as they remain sequestered in the philosophical community. They check their weapons at the door, as it were, and agree to tolerate one another in pursuit of self-knowledge while enjoying the process of tolerant interaction. It might seem, then, that the philosophical community is naïvely utopian. However, if that charge is supposed to mean that such communities do not exist, this is obviously false. Tolerant communities of philosophical inquiry exist wherever people 'do' philosophy: in a classroom, between friends, in the boardroom, or even, in quiet moments, on the battlefield. This is not to say that all friendships or classrooms (let alone all boardrooms or battlefields) are philosophical. Rather, the philosophical community occurs when we puzzle together, with friends, colleagues or comrades in arms.

But there is something right about the claim that the philosophical community is utopian. These communities do not possess material weapons – weapons stronger than words – with which to defend themselves against intolerance. This is why the philosophical community is tragic: it is always at risk from external enemies because philosophers are unwilling to use the same sorts of weapons against their enemies as their enemies are willing to use against them. At least, while doing philosophy, we agree not to use whatever material weapons we may have stashed in reserve for our inevitable return to the 'real' world; instead we use rhetorical and logical weapons, weapons that tend to be tolerant, but which are not immediately effective against those armed with material weapons. But the spirit of philosophy can extend beyond the philosophical utopia. When tolerant philosophers return to the 'real' world, they can bring the virtue of tolerance with them. This is a wonderful thing. Indeed, the social and political result of a widespread education in philosophy would be a marked increase in toleration in the real world.

We make our children more tolerant, in part, by encouraging them to think for themselves, to question authority and to pursue self-knowledge by listening tolerantly to others. In this, the heart of contemporary liberal education, we teach our children to become philosophers and to develop their own tolerant philosophical communities. We ask our children to become Socratic when we teach them to recognize their own ignorance, ethnocentrism and tendency towards subjective bias. We model their behaviour on that of Socrates when we demand that they refrain from violence and learn to speak critically and tolerantly to their antagonists. Of course this description of tolerant education is an ideal. Much of our educational practice, stultified and stymied by institutional necessities, falls far short of this ideal. Thus it does us good to consider and reconsider the models presented in this book as we each strive to lead an ethical life.

Notes

1. Plato, *Republic*, *The Collected Dialogues of Plato*, ed. Edith Hamilton and Huntingdon Cairns, Princeton, NJ: Princeton University Press, 1989, p. 534 b–c. See Alexander Nehamas' discussion in *Virtues of Authenticity*, Princeton, NJ: Princeton University Press, 1999, pp. 112–13.
2. Kant, *Critique of Pure Reason*, New York: St. Martin's Press, 1965, B 848.
3. Iris Marion Young, *Justice and the Politics of Difference*, Princeton, NJ: Princeton University Press, 1990, p. 114.
4. Alasdair MacIntyre, 'Toleration and the Goods of Conflict' in Susan Mendus (ed.) *The Politics of Toleration in Modern Life*, Durham, NC: Duke University Press, 2000, p. 138.
5. Catherine MacKinnon, *Toward A Feminist Theory of the State*, Cambridge, MA: Harvard University Press, 1989, p. 205.
6. John Rawls, *Justice as Fairness: A Restatement*, Cambridge, MA: Harvard University Press, 2001, p. 197.
7. See Andrew Fiala, *Practical Pacifism*, New York: Algora Publishing, 2004.
8. Michael Walzer, *Just and Unjust Wars*, New York: Basic Books, 1977.

Bibliography

Abraham, Susan, 'The Deorala Judgement Glorifying Sati' *http://www.hsph.harvard.edu/grhf/SAsia/forums/sati/articles/judgement.html*, accessed 2002.

Adorno, Theodore (1994) *Minima Moralia*. London: Verso.

Allen, R.T. (1989) 'When Loyalty No Harm Meant', *Review of Metaphysics*, 43(2):281–94.

Anderson, Thomas C. (1993) *Sartre's Two Ethics*. Chicago: Open Court Press.

Annas, Julia (1993) *The Morality of Happiness*. Oxford: Oxford University Press.

Apel, Karl-Otto (1997) 'Plurality of the Good?', *Ratio Juris*, 10(2):199–212.

Arendt, Hannah (1975) *The Origins of Totalitarianism*. New York: Harcourt Brace and Co.

Arendt, Hannah (1977) *Eichmann in Jerusalem*. New York: Penguin Books.

Aristotle (1985) *Nicomachean Ethics*. Indianapolis: Hackett Publishing.

Augustine (1961) *Confessions*. London: Collier Macmillan.

Baumann, Zygmunt (1997) *Postmodernity and Its Discontents*. New York: New York University Press.

Bauman, Zygmunt (2000) *Liquid Modernity*. Cambridge: Polity Press.

Beauchamp, Tom L. (1999) 'The Failure of Theories of Personhood', *Kennedy Institute of Ethics Journal*, 9(4):309–44.

Beauvoir, Simone de (1948) *The Ethics of Ambiguity*. Seacaucus, NJ: The Citadel Press.

Becker, Lawrence C. (1998) *A New Stoicism*. Princeton, NJ: Princeton University Press.

Beiner, Ronald (1992) *What's the Matter with Liberalism?* Berkeley, CA: University of California Press.

Bellah, Robert, *et al.* (1996) *Habits of the Heart*. Berkeley, CA: University of California Press.

Berlin, Isaiah (1969) *Four Essays on Liberty*. Oxford: Oxford University Press.

Blum, Lawrence (1998) 'Recognition, Value, and Equality: A Critique of Charles Taylor's and Nancy Fraser's Accounts of Multiculturalism' in Cynthia Willett (ed.) *Theorizing Multiculturalism*. Oxford: Blackwell.

Bobbio, Norberto (1996) 'In Praise of *La Mitezza*' in Paul Ricouer (ed.) *Tolerance Between Intolerance and the Intolerable* (an edition of *Diogenes*, no. 176, vol. 44/4, Winter 1996).

Bree, Germaine (1972) *Camus and Sartre: Crisis and Commitment*. New York: Delacorte Press.

Buber, Martin (1965) *The Knowledge of Man: Selected Essays*. New York: Harper and Row.

Cairns, Douglas L. (1993) *Aidos: The Psychology and Ethics of Honor and Shame in Ancient Greek Literature*. Oxford: Clarendon Press.

Camus, Albert (1986) *Neither Victims nor Executioners*. Philadelphia: New Society Publishers.

Camus, Albert (1991) *The Rebel*. New York: Vintage.

Camus, Albert (1995) *Resistance, Rebellion, and Death*. New York: Vintage.

Carrithers, Michael, Steven Collins and Steven Lukes (eds) (1985) *The Category of the Person: Anthropology, Philosophy, History*. Cambridge: Cambridge University Press.

Cicero (1929) *The Commonwealth*. Indianapolis: Bobbs Merrill Co.

Cicero (1961) *De Officiis*. Cambridge, MA: Harvard University Press.

Conway, Trudy (forthcoming) 'Tolerance and Hospitality', *Philosophy in the Contemporary World*.

Cook, John W. (1999) *Morality and Cultural Differences*. Oxford: Oxford University Press.

Cooper David E. (1990) *Existentialism*. Oxford: Basil Blackwell.

Creppell, Ingrid (1996) 'Locke on Toleration', *Political Theory*, 24(2):200–40.

Davidson, Donald (1982) 'On the Very Idea of a Conceptual Scheme' in Michael Krausz and Jack W. Meiland (eds) *Relativism: Cognitive and Moral*. Notre Dame, IN: University of Notre Dame Press.

Davies, J.K. (1978) *Democracy and Classical Greece*. Stanford, CA: Stanford University Press.

Descartes, Rene (1998) *Discourse on Method and Meditations on First Philosophy*. Indianapolis, IN: Hackett Publishing.

Dewey, John (1954) *The Public and its Problems*. New York: Henry Holt and Co.

Dewey, John (1957) *Reconstruction in Philosophy*. Boston: The Beacon Press.

Dewey, John (1984) *Individualism Old and New*, in John Dewey, *The Later Works* vol. 5. Carbondale, IL: Southern Illinois University Press.

Dewey, John (1987) *Liberalism and Social Action*, in John Dewey, *The Later Works* vol. 11. Carbondale, IL: Southern Illinois University Press.

Durant, Will (1944) *Caesar and Christ*. New York: Simon and Schuster.

Dworkin, Ronald (1996) 'Objectivity and Truth: You'd Better Believe It', *Philosophy and Public Affairs*, 25(2):87–139.

Dworkin, Ronald (2000) *Sovereign Virtue*. Cambridge, MA: Harvard University Press.

Elshtain, Jean Bethke (1995) *Democracy on Trial*. New York: Basic Books.

Emerson, Ralph Waldo (2000) *The Essential Writings of Ralph Waldo Emerson*. New York: Modern Library Classics.

Epictetus (1959) *Discourses*. Cambridge, MA: Harvard University Press.

Epictetus (1983) *The Handbook*. Indianapolis, IN: Hackett Publishing.

Estlund, David (1998) 'The Insularity of the Reasonable: Why Political Liberalism Must Admit the Truth', *Ethics*, 108(2):252–75.

Fiala, Andrew (2002) *The Philosopher's Voice*. Albany, NY: State University of New York Press.

Fiala, Andrew (2003) Introduction to Marcus Aurelius, *Meditations*. New York: Barnes and Noble.

Fiala, Andrew (2004) *Practical Pacifism*. New York: Algora Publishing.

Fraser, Nancy (1998) 'From Redistribution to Recognition? Dilemmas of Justice in a "Post-Socialist" Age' in Cynthia Willett (ed.) *Theorizing Multiculturalism*. Oxford: Blackwell.

Freud, Sigmund (1961) *Civilization and its Discontents*. New York: Norton.

Fromm Erich (1969) *Escape from Freedom*. New York: Avon Books.

Fukuyama Francis (1992) *The End of History and the Last Man*. New York: The Free Press.

Galeotti, Anna Elisabetta (2002) *Toleration as Recognition*. Cambridge: Cambridge University Press.

Gandhi, Mohandas K. (1993) *An Autobiography: The Story of My Experiments with Truth*. Boston: Beacon Press.

Gutmann, Amy (ed.) (1994) *Multiculturalism*. Princeton, NJ: Princeton University Press.

Gutting, Gary (1999) *Pragmatic Liberalism and the Critique of Modernity*. Cambridge: Cambridge University Press.

Hadas, Moses (ed.) (1958) *The Stoic Philosophy of Seneca*. New York: Doubleday Anchor.

Hadot, Pierre (2001) *The Inner Citadel: The Meditations of Marcus Aurelius*. Cambridge, MA: Harvard University Press.

Harrison, Geoffrey (1982) 'Relativism and Tolerance' in Michael Krausz and Jack W. Meiland (eds) *Relativism: Cognitive and Moral*. Notre Dame, IN: University of Notre Dame Press.

Hawley, John Stratton (1994) *Sati: The Blessing and the Curse*. Oxford: Oxford University Press.

Heidegger, Martin (1962) *Being and Time*. New York: Harper and Row.

Heidegger, Martin (1977) 'What is Metaphysics?' in David Farrell Krell (ed.) *Heidegger: Basic Writings*. San Francisco: Harper San Francisco.

Herman, Barbara (1996) 'Pluralism and the Community of Moral Judgment Virtue' in David Heyd (ed.) *Toleration: An Elusive Virtue*. Princeton, NJ: Princeton University Press.

Heyd, David (ed.) (1996) *Toleration: An Elusive Virtue*. Princeton, NJ: Princeton University Press.

Horton, John and Susan Mendus (1991) *John Locke: A Lettter Concerning Toleration in Focus*. London: Routledge.

Ignatieff, Michael (2000) 'Nationalism and Toleration' in Susan Mendus (ed.) *The Politics of Toleration in Modern Life*. Durham, NC: Duke University Press.

James, William (1964) 'The Will to Believe' in Walter Kaufmann (ed.) *Religion from Tolstoy to Camus*. New York: Harper Torchbooks.

James, William (1976) *Essays in Radical Empiricism*. Cambridge, MA: Harvard University Press.

James, William (1977) *A Pluralistic Universe*. Cambridge: Harvard University Press.

James, William (1983) *Talks to Teachers on Psychology and to Students on Some of Life's Ideals*. Cambridge, MA: Harvard University Press.

James, William (1994) *The Varieties of Religious Experience*. New York: The Modern Library.

John (1971) *Holy Bible* (Revised Standard Version). Dallas, TX: Melton Book Co.

Kant, Immanuel (1965) *Critique of Pure Reason*. New York: St Martin's Press.

Kaufmann, Walter (ed.) (1964) *Religion from Tolstoy to Camus*. New York: Harper Torchbooks.

Kekes, John (2000) *Pluralism in Philosophy: Changing the Subject*. Ithaca, NY: Cornell University Press.

Kierkegaard, Søren (1980) *The Sickness Unto Death*. Princeton, NJ: Princeton University Press, 1980.

Kim, Hye-Kyung and Michael Wreen (2003) 'Relativism, Absolutism, and Tolerance', *Metaphilosophy*, 34(4):447–59.

King, Preston (1998) *Toleration*, 2nd edition. London: Frank Cass.

Kloppenberg, James T. (1998) *The Virtues of Liberalism*. New York: Oxford University Press.

Krausz, Michael (2000) *The Limits of Rightness*. Lanham, MD: Rowman and Littlefield.

Krausz, Michael and Jack W. Meiland (eds) (1982) *Relativism: Cognitive and Moral*. Notre Dame, IN: University of Notre Dame Press.

Krell, David Farrell (ed.) (1977) *Heidegger: Basic Writings*. San Francisco: Harper San Francisco.

Kurtz, Paul (2000) *Embracing the Power of Humanism*. Lanham, MD: Rowman and Littlefield.

Kymlicka, Will (1989) 'Liberal Individualism and Liberal Neutrality', *Ethics*, 99(4):883–905, reprinted in James P. Sterba (ed.) *Justice: Alternative Political Perspectives*, 2nd edition, Belmont, CA: Wadsworth, 1992).

Kymlicka, Will (1989) *Liberalism, Community, and Culture*. Oxford: Clarendon Press.

Lachs, John (1995) *The Relevance of Philosophy to Life*. Nashville, TN: Vanderbilt University Press.

Lachs, John (2003) *A Community of Individuals*. New York: Routledge.

Laursen, John Christian (1996) 'Spinoza on Toleration' in Cary J. Nederman and John Christian Laursen (eds) *Difference and Dissent: Theories of Tolerance in Medieval and Early Modern Europe*. Lanham, MD: Rowman and Littlefield.

Levine, Alan (2001) *Sensual Philosophy: Toleration, Skepticism, and Montaigne's Politics of the Self*. Lanham, MD: Lexington Books.

Locke, John (1997) *A Letter Concerning Tolerance* in Steven M. Cahn (ed.) *Classics of Modern Political Theory*. New York: Oxford University Press.

MacIntyre, Alasdair (1981) *After Virtue*. Notre Dame, IN: University of Notre Dame Press.

MacIntyre, Alasdair (2000) 'Toleration and the Goods of Conflict' in Susan Mendus (ed.) *The Politics of Toleration in Modern Life*. Durham, NC: Duke University Press.

MacKinnon, Catherine (1989) *Toward A Feminist Theory of the State*. Cambridge, MA: Harvard University Press.

Mara, Gerald M. (1988) 'Socrates and Liberal Toleration', *Political Theory*, 16(3):468–95.

Marcel, Gabriel (1956) *Royce's Metaphysics*. Chicago: Henry Regnery Co.

Marcel, Gabriel (1963) *The Existential Background of Human Dignity*. Cambridge, MA: Harvard University Press.

Marcel, Gabriel (1967) *Man Against Mass Society*. Chicago: Henry Regnery Co.

Marcel, Gabriel (1979) *Mystery of Being: Faith and Reality*. Lanham, MD: University Press of America.

Marcel, Gabriel (1991) *The Philosophy of Existentialism*. New York: Citadel Press.

Marcel, Gabriel (2002) *Creative Fidelity*. New York: Fordham University Press.

Marcus Aurelius (1961) *The Communings with Himself of Marcus Aurelius Antoninus, Emperor of Rome*. Cambridge, MA: Harvard University Press.

Marcus Aurelius (1969) *Meditations*. Baltimore: Penguin.

Marcus Aurelius (2003) *Meditations*. New York: Barnes and Noble.

Marcuse, Herbert (1969) 'Repressive Tolerance' in Robert Wolff, Barrington Moore and Hebert Marcuse (eds) *A Critique of Pure Tolerance*. Boston: Beacon Press.

Margolis, Joseph (1986) *Pragmatism Without Foundations*. Oxford: Basil Blackwell.

Margolis, Joseph (1996) *Life Without Principles*. Cambridge, MA: Blackwell.

McCumber, John (1997) 'Aristotle and the Metaphysics of Intolerance' in Mehdi Amin Razavi and David Ambuel (eds) *Philosophy, Religion, and the Question of Intolerance*. Albany, NY: State University of New York Press.

Mendus, Susan (1989) *Toleration and the Limits of Liberalism*. Atlantic Highlands, NJ: Humanities Press International.

Mendus, Susan (1991) 'Locke: Toleration, Morality, and Rationality' in John Horton and Susan Mendus (eds) *John Locke: A Lettter Concerning Toleration in Focus*. London: Routledge.

Mendus, Susan (ed.) (2000) *The Politics of Toleration in Modern Life*. Durham, NC: Duke University Press.

Mendus, Susan and David Edwards (eds) (1987) *On Toleration*. Oxford: Clarendon Press.

Merleau-Ponty, Maurice (1969) *Humanism and Terror*. Boston: Beacon Press.

Merleau-Ponty, Maurice (1992) *Phenomenology of Perception*. London: Routledge.

Mill, John Stuart (1998) *On Liberty and Other Essays*. Oxford: Oxford World Classics.

Mitsis, Phillip (1999) 'The Stoic Origin of Natural Rights' in Katerina Ierodiakonou (ed.) *Topics in Stoic Philosophy*. Oxford: Oxford University Press.

Montaigne, Michel (1958) *Essays*. Stanford, CA: Stanford University Press.

Nagel, Thomas (1991) *Equality and Partiality*. Oxford: Oxford University Press.

Narasimhan, Sakuntala (1992) *Sati: Widow Burning in India*. New York: Anchor Books.

Nederman, Cary J. and John Christian Laursen (eds) (1996) *Difference and Dissent: Theories of Tolerance in Medieval and Early Modern Europe*. Lanham, MD: Rowman and Littlefield.

Nehamas, Alexander (1998) *The Art of Living*. Berkeley, CA: University of California Press.

Nehamas, Alexander (1999) *Virtues of Authenticity*. Princeton, NJ: Princeton University Press.

Newey, Glen (1999) *Virtue, Reason, and Toleration: The Place of Toleration in Ethical and Political Philosophy*. Edinburgh: University of Edinburgh Press.

Nietzsche, Friedrich (1968) *The Will to Power*. New York: Vintage Books.

Norton David (1996) *Imagination, Understanding, and the Virtue of Liberality*. Lanham, MD: Rowman and Littlefield.

Nussbaum, Martha C. (1994) *The Therapy of Desire*. Princeton, NJ: Princeton University Press.

Nussbaum, Martha C. (1997) *Cultivating Humanity*. Cambridge, MA: Harvard University Press.

Nussbaum, Martha C. (1997) 'Kant and Stoic Cosmopolitanism', *The Journal of Political Philosophy*, 5(1):1–25.

Nussbaum, Martha C. (2000) 'Aristotle, Politics, and Human Capabilities: A response to Antony, Arneson, Charlesworth, and Mulgan', *Ethics*, 111:102–40.

Nussbaum, Martha C. (2000) *Women and Human Development*. Cambridge: Cambridge University Press.

Nussbaum, Martha C. (2001) *Upheavals of Thought*. Cambridge: Cambridge University Press.

Oberdiek, Hans (2001) *Tolerance: Between Forbearance and Acceptance*. Lanham, MD: Rowman and Littlefield.

Parfit, Derek (1984) *Reasons and Persons*. Oxford: Clarendon Press.

Paterson, Orlando (1991) *Freedom*. New York: Basic Books.

Pihlström, Sami (2003) *Naturalizing the Transcendental*. New York: Humanity Books.

Plato (1989) *The Collected Dialogues of Plato*, ed. Edith Hamilton and Huntington Cairns. Princeton, NJ: Princeton University Press.

Pojman, Louis (2001) 'Who's to Judge' in Christina Sommers and Fred Sommers (eds) *Vice and Virtue in Everyday Life*, 5th edition. Fort Worth, TX: Harcourt College Publishers.

Popper, Karl (1971) *The Open Society and its Enemies*. Princeton, NJ: Princeton University Press.

Popper, Karl (1987) 'Toleration and Intellectual Responsibility' in Susan Mendus and David Edwards (eds) *On Toleration*. Oxford: Clarendon Press.

Rawls, John (1971) *A Theory of Justice*. Cambridge, MA: Harvard University Press.

Rawls, John (1995) 'Reply to Habermas', *Journal of Philosophy*, 92(3):132–80.

Rawls, John (1995) *Political Liberalism*. New York: Columbia University Press.

Rawls, John (1999) *The Law of Peoples*. Cambridge, MA: Harvard University Press.

Rawls, John (2001) *Justice as Fairness: A Restatement*. Cambridge, MA: Harvard University Press.

Razavi, Mehdi Amin and David Ambuel (eds) (1997) *Philosophy, Religion, and the Question of Intolerance*. Albany, NY: State University of New York Press, 1997.

Reiman, Jeffrey (1997) *Critical Moral Liberalism*. Lanham, MD: Rowman and Littlefield.

Ricouer, Paul (ed.) (1996) *Tolerance Between Intolerance and the Intolerable* (an edition of *Diogenes*, no. 176, vol. 44/4).

Rorty, Richard (1989) *Contingency, Irony, Solidarity*. Cambridge: Cambridge University Press.

Rosenthal, Michael A. (2001) 'Tolerance as a Virtue in Spinoza's Ethics', *Journal of the History of Philosophy*, 39(4):535–57.

Rousseau, Jean-Jacques (1967) *The Social Contract and Discourse on the Origin of Inequality*. New York: Washington Square Press.

Rousseau, Jean-Jacques (1979) *Emile*. New York: Basic Books.

Royce, Josiah (1959) *The World and the Individual*. New York: Dover Publications.

Royce, Josiah (1995) *Philosophy of Loyalty*. Nashville, TN: Vanderbilt University Press.

Rutherford, R.B. (1989) *The Meditations of Marcus Aurelius: A Study*. Oxford: Clarendon Press.

Sandbach, F.H. (1975) *The Stoics*. New York: Norton.

Sandel, Michael (1982) *Liberalism and the Limits of Justice*. Cambridge: Cambridge University Press.

Sandel, Michael (1996) *Democracy's Discontent*. Cambridge, MA: Harvard University Press.

Sartre, Jean-Paul (1956) *Being and Nothingness*. New York: Washington Square Press.

Sartre, Jean-Paul (1965) *Situations*. New York: George Braziller.

Sartre, Jean-Paul (1968) *Search for a Method*. New York: Vintage Books.

Sartre, Jean-Paul (1977) *Essays in Existentialism*. Seacausus, NJ: The Citadel Press.

Sartre, Jean-Paul (1992) *Truth and Existence*. Chicago: University of Chicago Press.

Seneca (1958) 'On Clemency' in Moses Hadas (ed.) *The Stoic Philosophy of Seneca*. New York: Doubleday Anchor.

Spinoza, Benedict (1951) *A Theologico-Political Treatise*. New York: Dover Publications.

Spinoza, Bendict (1993) *Ethics*. London: J.M. Dent Orion Publishing.

Sterba, James P. (ed.) (1992) *Justice: Alternative Political Perspectives*, 2nd edition. Belmont, CA: Wadsworth.

Tan, Kok-Chor (1998) 'Liberalism in Rawls' Law of Peoples', *Ethics*, 108(2):276–95.

Tan, Kok-Chor (2000) *Toleration, Diversity, and Global Justice*. University Park, PA: Pennsylvania State University Press.

Taylor, Charles (1985) 'The Person' in Carrithers, Collins and Lukes (eds) *The Category of the Person: Anthropology, Philosophy, History*. Cambridge: Cambridge University Press.

Taylor, Charles (1989) *Sources of the Self*. Cambridge, MA: Harvard University Press.

Taylor, Charles (1994) 'The Politics of Recognition' in Gutmann (ed.) *Multiculturalism*. Princeton, NJ: Princeton University Press.

Voltaire (1943) *Philosophical Dictionary*. Cleveland, OH: World Publishing Co.

Waldron, Jeremy (1991) 'Locke: Toleration and the Rationality of Persecution' in John Horton and Susan Mendus (eds) *John Locke: A Letter Concerning Toleration in Focus*. London: Routledge.

Walzer, Michael (1977) *Just and Unjust Wars*. New York: Basic Books.

Walzer, Michael (1983) *Spheres of Justice*. New York: Basic Books.

Walzer, Michael (1997) *On Toleration*. New Haven, CT: Yale University Press.

Weinberger-Thomas, Catherine (1999) *Ashes of Immortality: Widow Burning in India*. Chicago: University of Chicago.

Willett, Cynthia (ed.) (1998) *Theorizing Multiculturalism*. Oxford: Blackwell.

Williams Bernard (1996) 'Toleration: A Political or Moral Question' in Paul Ricouer (ed.) *Tolerance Between Intolerance and the Intolerable* (an edition of *Diogenes*, no. 176, vol. 44/4).

Williams, Bernard (1996) 'Toleration: An Impossible Virtue' in David Heyd (ed.) *Toleration: An Elusive Virtue*. Princeton, NJ: Princeton University Press.

Williams, Robert R. (1992) *Recognition: Fichte and Hegel on the Other*. Albany, NY: State University of New York Press.

Wolff, Robert, Barrington Moore and Hebert Marcuse (eds) (1969) *A Critique of Pure Tolerance*. Boston: Beacon Press.

Young, Iris Marion (1990) *Justice and the Politics of Difference*. Princeton, NJ: Princeton University Press.

Young, Iris Marion (1998) 'Unruly Categories: A Critique of Nancy Fraser's Dual Systems Theory' in Cynthia Willett (ed.) *Theorizing Multiculturalism*. Oxford: Blackwell.

Žižek, Slavoj (2002) 'A Plea for Leninist Intolerance', *Critical Inquiry*, 28:542–66.

Index